Inspirations In the Key of "J"

Judy Miller

authorHOUSE®

AuthorHouse™
1663 Liberty Drive, Suite 200
Bloomington, IN 47403
www.authorhouse.com
Phone: 1-800-839-8640

First published by AuthorHouse 5/20/2008

ISBN: 978-1-4343-7862-0 (sc)

Printed in the United States of America
Bloomington, Indiana

This book is printed on acid-free paper.

For the piano music CD, email Judy at gjmiller@telusplanet.net
Cost is $9.95 including shipping.

Acknowledgements

As I sit here and think about a book being printed that I have penned, I feel very humbled. As you read through the devotionals for the next few months, you will see bits and pieces of my story. God has been writing my story from the day I was born—even before I was born. That, in itself, is humbling. He knew who my parents would be; He knew who my grandparents would be; He brought my Mom and my Dad together. He knew the choices they would make. He knew the choices I would make.

Pondering these things, I would like to acknowledge my parents, Jacob and Dorothy Heide. I would like to lift them up, and exalt them for being the wonderful parents they were to me. If it wasn't for them, I wouldn't be who I am today. They brought me up in a Christian home. My Dad passed on his gentle, quiet nature to me. How I remember well my Dad's hugs, my Dad always saying, "I love you, honey" at the end of the day. In fact, those were the last words I heard my Dad say to me. My Mom passed on her ability to laugh, and to encourage others. Oh, how she loved to entertain, and make others feel welcome in our home. Anything I have written in these devotionals, I know that my parents would be excited that I have shared these few little experiences with you, the reader. They will be praising God if one little thing I have written has helped you to look at yourselves, and to grow a little closer to God because of it.

I would like to acknowledge others as well. If it weren't for my husband, Graham, I would not have been able to write these devotionals. Thanks, honey, for your support. Also, my children, Warren, Roxanne, Shandra and Joan. I have learned so many things from my children, and my grandchildren. It has been an interesting journey of learning and unlearning as the years go by. I delight in my grown children, and am so thankful for them, and their love for me. A special thanks to Shandra for helping me with the formatting of this book.

Thanks to Ron Hatton, an author from Tennessee, who planted the seed of printing a book with my devotionals. He graciously allowed me to use the title that he suggested, "Inspirations in the Key of "J" ".

The music CD—Anthony Burger, from the Gaither Vocal Band, said that his goal in playing the piano was that the listeners would hear the words. That is my goal as well. Marcel Frey helped in making this CD—as well as Wade Dedio. Thanks, guys. Without you, it would have not happened. Many friends (too numerous to mention) helped me find the music I wanted. Thanks.

I give God all the honor, and praise, and glory for what He has done in my life.

Let's praise God together. The joy of the Lord is my strength!

Contents

A Good Example

Matthew 9:9 And as Jesus passed forth from thence, he saw a man, named Matthew, sitting at the receipt of custom: and he saith unto him, Follow me. And he arose, and followed him. (KJV)

The other day when we were in the mall, I saw a tiny little girl walking by herself. I was concerned so looked around for a parent. Sure enough, there was her Daddy a few feet in front of her walking slowly. After a short time, he turned and walked backwards, I'm sure to make certain she was still following him. When she saw him turn around, she did the same thing, now walking backwards as she followed him. The Dad, smiling broadly, turned and walked front wards again. Soon, the little daughter turned and walked front wards as well. The tiny little girl had her eyes on her Dad and followed his every move.

Seeing the little girl with her Dad reminded me of Matthew in today's Scripture. We are to rise up and follow Jesus. We can accomplish this by spending time reading God's Word, studying it, meditating on it, and applying the principles we learn to our lives. Let's follow Jesus every step of the way.

Prayer Lord Jesus, deep in our hearts, we want to become more like You. Help us to keep our eyes on You and follow in Your every footstep. Amen

---

My Thoughts

Sept 2. 2008

Today I had more energy.
I delivered some papers. did yoga
watered Angys plants had breakfast
Thank you Lord for this energy.

Lord let me keep my eyes on
you today het me be a blessing
to others, het me not take
my husband for granted just because
his here het me show him my love
and support and dear Lord I pray. I
will not try to controll him in any
way. Lord you know my heart keep
it pure for you.

Mary Ann = Heman are comming
today. Lord I pray for energy
today so they will know they are
so welcome.

Nehemiah 8:10
Don't be dejected and sad, for
the joy of the Lord is your strength

7

A Little Birdie Told Me

1 Chronicles 28:9 "And you, Solomon my son, get to know well your father's God; serve him with a whole heart and eager mind, for GOD examines every heart and sees through every motive. (MSG)

As a child, there were many times that I would do something that I thought my mother knew nothing about—you know the good, the bad and the ugly. Sometimes, I thought I had gotten away with one of the bad things—for a few days. Then Mom would say she knew about it. When I was very young, I couldn't understand how she knew. She often said, "A little birdie told me." I couldn't understand where that little birdie was or how he could talk and tell Mom those things. When I questioned her about it, she would often say that she had eyes in the back of her head. That made no sense to me either.

Of course, as I grew, I knew who the birdie was. Also, as a mother, I understood about having eyes in the back of my head. I had them too. I also had a little birdie in my home when my children were young.

I have thought about those experiences in relation to today's verse of Scripture. God does see what we do—the good, the bad and the ugly. But more than that, He examines our hearts and sees through our every motive. Nothing is hidden from Him. That is a sobering thought.

Are our motives right when we serve others? Are they right when we serve God? How about with our work? Our careers? Our friends? Our family? What is God seeing when He is examining our hearts? In today's verse, King David is admonishing his son to get to know God and to serve Him whole heartedly. When we get to know God, then we can be more aware of our motives. We can hear God admonish us more easily when our motives are wrong. Let's pursue Him with our whole heart, soul and mind and strength.

Prayer Lord Jesus, thank You for this admonition to get to know You and to serve You. Please show us what is deep in our hearts. Sometimes, we don't even know our motives. But You do and we thank You for that. May we be ready and willing to listen to You in every area of our lives. Amen

---

My Thoughts

Sept 9/08

Just think! God knows
our every thought and motive.
Its pretty scary.

My verse has been, hard,
create in me a clean heart
Lord, I pray that my
motives will be worthy.

I pray you will forgive
any unclean thoughts I have.
Let me start today with
joy in my heart for you.

Thankyou for extra energy.

Wendy + Gilbert were here
last week, enjoyed their company.

George will be comming
today if all goes well with
his agenda.

My blessing for today.
to be able to get
up a little earlier to
do a study. Thankyou Lord

A Little Bit of Heaven

1 Chronicles 29:11 To you, O GOD, belong the greatness and the might, the glory, the victory, the majesty, the splendor; Yes! Everything in heaven, everything on earth; the kingdom all yours! You've raised yourself high over all. (MSG)

I grew up in southern Alberta, Canada. On rare occasions on a cold winter night, we could see the Aurora Borealis, or more commonly known as the northern lights.

After moving to northern Alberta, we were shocked to be able to see the same spectacular view all year long. Because the days here in the summer are very long, we have to stay up very late to see them. The first year, we would lay out on the lawn and watch, enthralled with the dancing lights all over the sky. They are always white, but often yellows, greens, and pinks as well. It is a sight to behold.

We are quite used to seeing them all year round now. But when our International students come, that is one highlight they don't want to miss. They will stay up very late night after night in order to see them.

We like to think that the Aurora Borealis is a little glimpse of Jesus and heaven. God is allowing us to see a teeny bit of the majesty and glory and magnificence of our eternal home.

Prayer Thank You, Father God, for the beautiful northern lights. They are breath taking at times. How much grander heaven will be! Amen

---

My Thoughts

A New Year

<u>Romans 7:19</u> I decide to do good, but I don't really do it; I decide not to do bad, but then I do it anyway. (MSG)

A new year has dawned upon us. On my wall hangs a new calendar. Each year, I get calendars made. Pictures of our family are on each month's page. As I look at January, our whole family is there smiling back at me. I wonder what is in store for all of us this year. Will we grow closer together as a family? Will there be some clashes that we have to work through? What will those clashes look like?

Beneath the picture hangs the new month of January. On a few of the dates, I have written family's birthdays. Other than that, the whole month is clean and white and unspotted. What will it look like by the end of the month? We have choices to make each and every day of that month. That will determine what will be on that page. Will there be sins? Failures? Victories? Triumphs? Sympathy shown to us and to others? Understanding? Love extended? A breakthrough in a relationship? A stronghold broken? Forgiveness? A death of someone dear to us? When we look back at each month as the year progresses, will we see growth? Will we see set backs?

<u>Romans 7:24-25</u> I've tried everything and nothing helps. I'm at the end of my rope. Is there no one who can do anything for me? Isn't that the real question? The answer, thank God, is that Jesus Christ can and does. He acted to set things right in this life of contradictions where I want to serve God with all my heart and mind, but am pulled by the influence of sin to do something totally different. (MSG)

Let's choose to commit each day to the Lord. We can't do it ourselves. Even when we want to do good, we don't, and when we don't want to do evil, we do. Thank God, through Jesus Christ, we can live victoriously.

> Prayer Lord Jesus, as this new year unfolds before us, help us to let go and let God. We can't live life successfully by our own strength. Help us to admit we can't do anything without You. Help us to invite You into every area of our lives. Help us not to be discouraged when we do err. You are so willing to forgive us, and to give us a clean page on which to start over. Thank You. Amen

My Thoughts

A Short Road Home

<u>Luke 15:20</u> "So he went at once to his father. While he was still at a distance, his father saw him and felt sorry for him. He ran to his son, put his arms around him, and kissed him. (GW)

When I was a child and we would go about seven or eight miles to visit some friends, I thought it took forever to arrive at their home. This was a country gravel road, so my Dad never drove as fast as on the paved highway.

On the way back home, it didn't seem to me to take long to get home at all. I remember commenting to my Mom about it. She said that it is always nice to go home and that is why it didn't seem to take as long.

I have thought about that in a spiritual sense recently. Sometimes, we wander far from God. When we get to our destination and look back at where we have come from, we can see that the road was long; it was hard; it was bumpy; it was rough. When we realize how far we have wandered, we turn and run back to God, like the prodigal son did. The father was waiting for him—he saw him coming from a long way off. The father ran to meet his son and welcome him home.

I wonder if the road was long for the son to make to go back home. Was he wondering what his father's reaction to him would be? Would he be judged? Would he be condemned? Would he be accepted? The father was eagerly waiting and watching for him to return.

God, our Father, is waiting for us with welcoming arms. His child has come home. Oh, to relax in His arms, knowing He loves and cares for us, and forgives us! The journey back really isn't so long after all.

> *Prayer Lord Jesus, thank You for watching for us to return to You. Often, in our day-to-day lives, we stray, but You are waiting for us with open arms to welcome us back home. How we praise You for that today! Amen*

My Thoughts

Alaska

Psalms 16:11 Thou wilt show me the path of life: in thy presence is fullness of joy; at thy right hand there are pleasures forevermore. (KJRV)

We all know that Alaska is north. Well, in our city, we have a sign that say, "West – Alaska". How can that be? Should we trust it? You see the further north we drive in Canada, the fewer roads there are; hence, one road to Alaska from here. We must keep our eyes open to see the signs along the highway as we journey on to arrive at our desired destination. So to get to Alaska, we first have to see the sign that says to go west. Further on down the highway, there is a sign pointing north to Alaska. We do trust the traffic signs we see along the way. I wonder if those traveling there want to turn around and come back after they have driven through miles and miles of forest. There are many days of traveling, many miles to pass over, and many bridges to cross. I am told the beauty of Alaska is well worth the time and effort to go there.

In today's Scripture verse, it talks about fullness of joy in God's presence and pleasures forever at His right hand. That is such a blessed thought. We have days of traveling on that path, too. We have many bridges to cross. Often, we get weary. Often, the drudgeries of life discourage us. Often, the mountains in life bring us to despair. Just like driving to Alaska and watching for the signs, we need to keep our eyes open and on the Lord, following His every step.

Let's keep our eyes on God's Word when He says that He will show us the path of life. It is a promise that He has given us. The fullness of joy and pleasures forever will be worth it.

> _Prayer_   _Lord Jesus, so many times life is a challenge. We start off full of energy, but sometimes we just want to kick up our heels and quit. We lose sight of Your path for us. Help us to keep our eyes on You. Help us to lean on Your promise of pleasures forever and fullness of joy. Amen_

My Thoughts

Ant Hills

Galatians 5:13 For you were called to freedom, brethren; only do not turn your freedom into an opportunity for the flesh, but through love serve one another. (NASB)

This year we had a big ant hill in our back alley. Those little ants fascinate me. As I watched them, it seemed to me that they were just running every which way, back and forth, with no purpose.

I know that they do have a purpose. Even though I couldn't see it, I also know that there is team work in an ant hill. As I was looking around, I discovered a smaller ant hill a short distance away. Just recently, it has been brought to my attention that there is a larger ant hill across the back alley. I wondered if ant hills get to a certain size, and then, some go off to start another home—still connected to the larger home, though.

I saw a picture of our church there in the back alley. It is so large, we can't possibly know everyone. We can't feel connected because of the number of people. Therefore, we have many small groups getting together every day of the week, through which we can connect with a few people. We are a group to serve one another, and encourage one another. How great it is to feel we belong. By being connected to a few, we are connected to the whole.

How are we doing in the area of serving? Do we feel we belong in our church? I would like to suggest that by serving one another in love, we will feel like we belong.

Prayer Thank You for our church, Lord Jesus. Thank You for small groups where we can feel connected in a large group of people. Help us to serve one another in love. By doing so, we do feel connected. Amen

My Thoughts

Are We Following the Right Light?

John 8:12 Jesus once again addressed them: "I am the world's Light. (MSG)

Years ago, I had a kitten that I loved. It was so much fun to watch her. When we threw a candy wrapper across the room, she would bring it back to us. The game could go on all evening long.

I have an anniversary clock on which the sun shines at times during the day. When the sun shines on the turning parts, it reflects lights on the wall. It wasn't long until Kitty saw that, and would chase them back and forth, back and forth, for hours. If they were too high for her to attempt catching, she would jump at them on the wall. I loved watching her do that.

I have thought about that. She was chasing a light. Kitty didn't know what that light was. All she knew was that something was moving back and forth, and true to her feline instincts, she chased it. She never did catch it though, for as soon as she got to it, it would move, and away she would go again.

John 1:43 Jesus decided to go to Galilee…he ran across Philip and said, "Come, follow me." (MSG)

In our spiritual lives, we do know what the Light is, or I should say we do know *Who* the light is. Jesus is that Light Whom we are to follow. Wherever He goes, we are to go. The Light leads us, just like the star led the shepherds those many years ago. Oh, may we ever be conscious of seeing the Light and following it!

There are times, though, that we see another light and chase after it like Kitty did. We just can never quite catch it, but it is fun trying. It is so futile to chase after the things in this world that can't satisfy our hungry souls.

I would like to suggest that we chase after The Light of the world and follow Him. He will supply our every need—spiritually, emotionally, physically. (Philippians 4:19)

> *Prayer Lord Jesus, You are the Light of the world. Help us to ever keep our eyes on You and to follow You with a willing heart. You have promised to supply our every need. Help us to trust You to do so. Amen*

My Thoughts

Arms

Deuteronomy 33:27 The eternal God is thy refuge, and underneath are the everlasting arms. (NKJV)

When we moved to Grande Prairie, Alberta, Canada, seventeen years ago, one thing I hadn't seen before was a logging truck—one of those big trucks that hauls trees from the forest to the lumber mill. I was from the bald-headed prairie, where there were no trees to cut down and haul away.

These trucks are huge. The trees on them are huge. There are many logs on one loaded truck. Some are longer than others. Some are rougher than others. Some are a different color. These trucks are taking the logs to a mill where they will be made into useable lumber, into paper, into pencils, into numerous items that are useful to us. What holds the trees on the trucks are big steel arms, on each side. Those arms are strong. They have to be, in order to hold that many huge trees.

Jesus' arms hold us. Do we see the likeness between the logging trucks and the Lord's arms holding us? Some of us are rough—with harshness spewing out of our mouths. Some of us have parts that have been with us a long time—like grudges. Some are a different color, or turn a different color, showing our anger or jealousy. But Jesus' arms are holding us strongly—no matter what we are like. He loves us, and cares for us, and is carrying us to the place where we will be made into something more useful than we are now. His arms are strong enough to carry us to our final destination with Him in glory. Praise His Name!

> *Prayer Thank You, Lord Jesus, for Your strong arms. Thank You that You carry us along life's road to places where we will change to become more like You. You will take Your people to heaven to be with You. Help us to rest confidently in Your arms today. Amen*

My Thoughts

Arrival Day

<u>Matthew 28:19-20</u> Therefore, go and make disciples of all nations, baptizing them in the name of the Father and the Son and the Holy Spirit. Teach these new disciples to obey all the commands I have given you. And be sure of this; I am with you always, even to the end of the age. (NLT)

Recently, I was expecting an international student to arrive here in Grande Prairie, Alberta, Canada. Before she came, she emailed me, so I would know what day to be at the airport, what time to be there, and the number of the flight on which she was due to arrive.

While I was waiting for the passengers to enter the terminal, I saw a mother and daughter come through the doors. They had been on a journey, and were obviously glad to be home. The mother's eyes searched the crowd, found her husband, and fastened on him, who came over and hugged and kissed her tenderly. Then, he immediately hugged his daughter, as his wife's eyes also turned to the daughter. I'm sure they were all anxious to see each other.

I thought about the day when we arrive in heaven. Our eyes will be fastened on Jesus, and He will be waiting for us. He knows our arrival day, our arrival time, and our flight number. He will welcome us home. I wonder if He'll be looking to see if we brought anyone with us, like the husband looked for his daughter. The event at the air terminal made tears come to my eyes—especially when I thought about the eternal picture.

Will we bring others with us to Heaven? Will we bring our children to Heaven? Our grandchildren? Our neighbors? Our friends? It is a sobering thought.

Prayer Lord Jesus, You have told us to go and make disciples. Yet so often, when You nudge us to talk to others about You, we push the thought aside. Often we are filled with fear. Your Word says that You have "not given us the spirit of fear and timidity, but of power, love and a self discipline". (2 Timothy 1:7 NLT) Please help us. Thank You. Amen

My Thoughts

Be Still

Psalms 46:10 Be still and know that I am God. (NIV)

I have a remote starter on my car. It has many purposes. It will start and turn off the motor. It will lock and unlock the doors. When it does this, the horn honks – once or twice – depending on whether it is being locked or unlocked. It will open the trunk. It will arm the alarm system, and when it is triggered, the car's horn will blow continually until I use the remote to turn it off. Maybe there are more uses of which I am unaware.

Recently I have discovered another use for my car starter – a use that is not in the owner's manual. One day I came out of the store into a large parking lot, and realized that I had no idea where the car was. I headed off in the general direction that I thought it was, only to discover it wasn't there. So I headed another direction. To my dismay, it wasn't there either. Then, I remembered that the horn blows when I press a button on my remote. So I pressed the button. Because of the traffic noise, I had to tune in and listen carefully to hear the right sound. I had to be still. I did hear it in the distance, and so went that direction. I still couldn't locate my car anywhere so pressed the button again. This time, the sound came from behind me – opposite to where I was originally heading. This continued for quite a while. I got the giggles about it. I kept wandering around the parking lot, laughing and continuing to follow the sound of the horn – back and forth. Finally, to my great relief, I found the car. If it wasn't for my ears and ability to hear, I might still be there wandering around looking for my car!

What voices do we hear in our lives? The voice of God? Are our ears tuned into hearing what God has to say to us? Do we immediately head that direction, like I did with the horn on my car? That is God's desire for our lives. Jesus Christ is waiting for us to be still and listen carefully to Him and His teachings.

Prayer Dear Jesus, so many times, our ears aren't tuned to You. But You want to speak to us in Your soft, gentle voice. Often there is too much noise going on in us and around us. If only we will sit still, You will often whisper to us. Help us to hear and to listen to what You have to say to us. Amen

My Thoughts

Blooming

Philippians 1:6 Being confident of this, that he who began a good work in you will carry it on to completion until the day of Christ Jesus. (NIV)

I have many peony plants in my flower beds. Each one has special meaning. Two I have in memory of my Dad who passed away a few years ago. One is in memory of Mom who has been gone for many years. Still another was given to me by my mother-in-law. The rest I dug from the flower garden of one of my best friends, who has since moved away. I love my peonies. The blossoms have been huge this year. They are beautiful.

While there were still buds on the plants, I was anticipating the day when they would be in full bloom. I kept watching daily. On a really hot day, I could almost see some of them opening as the day progressed.

I thought about how they are so much like us. God's desire is for us to bloom. We do open up bit by bit like the peonies. Some of us bloom quickly. Some of us bloom more slowly. I wonder if those of us who are enduring some heat (like my peonies on that hot day) bloom more quickly. Heat can come in many forms—a misunderstanding in a relationship, the death of someone near to us, a wayward dear friend or family member, an accident, or health problems, to name a few.

I believe God allows some heat in our lives to help us to bloom. That is His work in our hearts, and He will continue to do so until we see Him face to face in glory.

> _Prayer Lord Jesus, thank You for the flowers that You have made for us to enjoy. When we see them blooming, may we ever be mindful of Your purpose in our lives. Help us to look beyond the heat, knowing You are helping us to bloom. You are building character in us. Help us to relax in that knowledge, knowing that as buds, we are opening more and more each day. Thank You. Amen_

My Thoughts

Blooming Again

1 Peter 5:7 Live carefree before God; he is most careful with you. (MSG)

Matthew 11:28-30 "Are you tired? Worn out? Burned out on religion? Come to me. Get away with me and you'll recover your life. I'll show you how to take a real rest. Walk with me and work with me—watch how I do it. Learn the unforced rhythms of grace. I won't lay anything heavy or ill-fitting on you. Keep company with me and you'll learn to live freely and lightly." (MSG)

A couple of weeks ago, we had some down pours and a bit of hail a few days in a row. My poor petunias looked pretty sick. The beautiful blossoms were all beaten off by the rain and hail. It almost made me cry. I picked off all the dead, crushed flowers and threw them away. The flowers have no choice in what happens to them in the flower garden.

Within a couple of days, when the sun was shining warmly, the petunias burst forth in new, full bloom, with every color of the rainbow. How beautiful they were. As I looked at them, I knew they needed the rain to grow. I also knew they needed the sunshine.

In our lives, when we get rained on and hailed on, it is not our choice either. We may feel we can't go on any longer or any further. We can't take one more step. If we allow Jesus to come and take the dead flowers away in our lives, He will gladly do that. He wants to take away the self-serving, the pride, the self-sufficiency. Then, if we allow the Son to shine His warmth into our battered hearts, we will bloom again. It won't take long, and Jesus' beauty will be revealed in us. Praise His name.

> *Prayer Thank You, dear Jesus, for the storms in life. Sometimes we get discouraged because it storms so often. We feel like giving up. But we do need to be watered and we do need the Sonshine. Help us, O Lord, we pray. Amen*

My Thoughts

Blueberries

Galatians 5:22-23 But the fruit of the Spirit is love, joy, peace, longsuffering, gentleness, goodness, faith, meekness, temperance: against such there is no law. (KJVR)

Romans 8:28 That's why we can be so sure that every detail in our lives of love for God is worked into something good. (MSG)

Apparently, if a person knows where to go around Grande Prairie, Alberta, Canada, you can find wonderful blueberry patches, where you can fill your buckets in no time at all.

Quite a few years ago, a forest fire went through that area. The regular blueberry pickers were so disappointed that the bushes had been burned, and there would be none to pick. I'm not sure how long it took, but eventually, the bushes did grow. The blueberries were even bigger, and sweeter, and more plenteous than before. I have asked the old timers in our area what caused that. They say it was because of the fire that the bushes produced so much better. We don't understand that principle, but it is true.

I see a likeness to our lives here. As Christians, we do produce fruit. It is a given, according to today's Scripture verse. In people's lives, I have also seen more fruit, more plenteous, and sweeter fruit being produced. It most often comes because the person has gone through some fire—just like the blueberry bushes. Sometimes, it takes a short time to produce more fruit. Sometimes, it takes a long time. God is working all of it for good.

Psalms 37:7 Rest in the LORD, and wait patiently for him. (KJVR)

When we're going through the fires of life, may we cling to God's promises, trusting Him to produce more abundant, and sweeter fruit.

> *Prayer Lord Jesus, we can learn so many things from nature. Every time we see blueberries, may we trust You more, cling to You more, wait for You more. Amen*

My Thoughts

Boy, That's Good, Ain't It?

I remember well my childhood when money was hard to come by. Bread bought in a store was a luxury; cookies from the store were a treat; an ice cream cone was almost unheard of; a Dixie cup eaten with a little wooden spoon – well, I thought I was in heaven.

One summer afternoon, my mom, her mom, my sister and I were in town. It was a very hot day. We had been working hard – likely picking peas or beans and freezing them, weeding in the garden, or maybe butchering chickens in the morning. Whatever it was, after lunch, we cleaned up and went to town for the weekly grocery shopping spree.

While we were there, my mom suggested we go into a little café and have a glass of pop. Well, just the mention of it was a delight to a little girl's heart. In we went. We all ordered orange pop. As we sat and sipped it slowly to prolong the special occasion, my grandma said, "Boy, that's good, ain't it?" We all agreed and kept sipping slowly. It was so refreshing on such a hot day.

I have thought about that event recently. As I read God's Word, I can say, "Boy, that's good, ain't it?"

John 3:16 This is how much God loved the world: He gave his Son, his one and only Son. And this is why: so that no one need be destroyed; by believing in him, anyone can have a whole and lasting life. (MSG)

Boy, that's good, ain't it?

Galatians 5:1 Christ has set us free to live a free life. So take your stand! Never again let anyone put a harness of slavery on you. (MSG)

Boy, that's good, ain't it?

Psalms 34:17-18 Is anyone crying for help? GOD is listening, ready to rescue you. If your heart is broken, you'll find GOD right there; if you're kicked in the gut, he'll help you catch your breath. (MSG)

Boy, that's good, ain't it?

There are so many promises in God's Word for us. Let's read it and claim these truths as ours.

> Prayer Lord Jesus, so many times we read Your Word, skipping over it quickly. Speak to us as we read Your Word today. Help us to find a "Boy, that's good, ain't it?" truth. Amen

My Thoughts

Broken Limbs

1 Peter 5:10 After you have suffered for a little while, the God of all grace, who called you to His eternal glory in Christ, will Himself perfect, confirm, strength and establish you. (NASB)

Psalms 138:8 The LORD will perfect that which concerneth me: thy mercy, O LORD, endureth forever: forsake not the works of thine own hands. (KJVR)

I saw a lady the other day with a cast on her leg, hobbling along on crutches. I wondered how she had broken her leg. I thought of the pain in which she would have been. And how long was it before she got to the hospital? How much pain killer did she need? And for how long? X-rays would have been taken at the hospital. The physician would have viewed those x-rays to confirm the break. Then he would have set the broken bones in the correct position before the cast was applied. That way the bones would not be moving while they were healing. The bones were put in the perfect position. They were established in order to be strengthened.

So many times in our lives, we have a broken bone somewhere—it could be a broken friendship, a broken marriage, a broken church relationship. We hurt, and we suffer a while. In today's Scripture verse, it says that God confirms that we are in pain. He doesn't deny it, nor does He want us to deny it. He will perfect that which concerns us. He will strengthen us. He will establish us. He will not forsake us. Thank You, Jesus.

Prayer Lord Jesus, life hurts. It hurts really badly sometimes. And sometimes, it lasts for a very long time. You see our pain. Thank You that You understand. Thank You that You will perfect those times, those things in our lives that cause us so much pain. Help us to trust You in those difficult times, knowing that You will strengthen us. Amen

---

My Thoughts

Call to Me

Psalms 37:4-5 Delight yourself in the LORD; And He will give you the desires of your heart. Commit your way to the LORD, Trust also in Him, and He will do it. (NASB)

Philippians 4:19 You can be sure that God will take care of everything you need, his generosity exceeding even yours in the glory that pours from Jesus. (MSG)

Jeremiah 33:3 'Call to me and I will answer you. I'll tell you marvelous and wondrous things that you could never figure out on your own.' (MSG)

I don't dream often but recently I had a dream that was so real. It was kind of mixed up like dreams are, but such a message in this dream.

After visiting with a friend in her home, I went to drive home. I could see the car across the street, but at the same time, it was in a huge parking lot. I searched for my car for hours. I was totally exhausted. Finally, I cried out to God, saying I was helpless to find my car, and I needed Him. As clear as can be, I heard God say, "Yes, you do need Me. I will help you!" What a relief!

The next thing I heard Him say was this, "You are helpless to overcome your addiction. You can't do it in your own strength, but I will help you!"

You see, I have an addiction – an addiction to food –the comfort foods like breads, desserts, peanut butter. I chase after them to fill my need.

This dream was so impressive, and so dramatic, and so real. When I awoke, I was comforted. I knew God was willing and able to help me overcome my addiction.

Jesus Christ wants to be our strength. He wants to meet all of our needs; the only way for Him to do that is for us to ask Him, and to trust Him to do as He says.

Prayer Thank You, Lord Jesus, for speaking to us in dreams. Thank You that You promise to meet all of our needs. So many times, we try to fill that void with other things—things like food, drugs, toys, busyness and work. You want to be the center of our lives. Help us to recognize our neediness and run to You with our emptiness for You to fill. Amen

My Thoughts

Changes

Ecclesiastes 3:1 There is an appointed time for everything. And there is a time for every event under heaven. (NASB)

This summer, the temperatures have been very rare for our part of Canada. We are breaking record highs a few days in a row. It has been over thirty degrees Celsius often. A few days ago, I saw on the weather network that it was to remain hot all week. Then, on Saturday, the high was to be nine degrees Celsius. What a change! That would feel like winter after being so hot for so long. Then it was to get really hot again. What changes! And so quickly!

We have changes in our lives as well—some do come quickly—like the death of a close relative, or a sickness that occurs suddenly, or our children moving out and leaving the empty nest for us to deal with. Other changes are slower—like cancer, gradually affecting our bodies year after year, or our children growing and becoming more independent as each day passes.

Psalms 37:7 Rest in the LORD and wait patiently for Him. (NASB)

Psalms 100:1-5 Shout joyfully to the LORD, all the earth. Serve the LORD with gladness; Come before Him with joyful singing. Know that the LORD Himself is God; It is He who has made us, and not we ourselves; We are His people and the sheep of His pasture. Enter His gates with thanksgiving and His courts with praise. Give thanks to Him, bless His name. For the LORD is good; His lovingkindness is everlasting and His faithfulness to all generations. (NASB)

Change is inevitable. Some change is good, and welcomed. Some change is hard to accept. How do we deal with it? We rest in the Lord. We shout joyfully to the Lord. We trust that He has made us. We trust that we are His. We give thanks. We trust that the Lord is good. We trust that His lovingkindness is everlasting, and He is faithful.

Prayer Lord Jesus, we don't like change. On the whole, we resist change—whether it comes slowly or quickly. Help us to trust You completely in the times of change in our lives. Thank You. Amen

---

My Thoughts

Choice to Rejoice

Philippians 4:4   Rejoice in the Lord always: and again I say, Rejoice. (NKJV)

James 1:2-3 My brethren, count it all joy when ye fall into divers temptations; Knowing this, that the trying of your faith worketh patience. (NKJV)

Years ago, I was discouraged and depressed. Life was rough. Every where I turned, it seemed that nothing improved. In fact, at times, it seemed to get worse. It was then that I started going for counseling and attending church again after many years of not going. One sermon was so meaningful to me. The pastor spoke about counting it all joy when going through rough times. I wondered how I could do that.

In our verse from Philippians today, it is a command to rejoice. We are to rejoice in the Lord – not just rejoice. God does give us a choice: we can choose to obey God or to disobey God. Then in the verse from James, I saw the truth that the struggles we go through bring patience into our lives. Some good is brought about because of the trying of our faith. Once I saw that, it was easier to rejoice. It was easier to trust that God knew what He was talking about.

I decided to try it and have found that God's Word is true—once again. It is hard to rejoice when things are rough. It is even hard to _think_ about rejoicing. But, oh, do we want to be obedient children or disobedient children?

Prayer   Dear God, how do we rejoice when things are tough in our lives? Help us to see beyond those things. Help us to see Your goodness and kindness to us. It is then that we can rejoice in You and You alone. The tough times then diminish in their stature and You increase. Just like John the Baptist said, "You must increase but we must decrease". (John 3:30) When we rejoice in You, You do increase. Thank you, Father. Amen

---

My Thoughts

Christmas Gifts

Luke 2:11 For today in the city of David there has been born for you a Savior, who is Christ the Lord. (NASB)

1 Thessalonians 5:18 Thank God no matter what happens. This is the way God wants you who belong to Christ Jesus to live. (MSG)

I remember Christmas past very well. A few days before Christmas, we would decorate a real live Christmas tree that was about five or six feet tall. My brother was very particular about how the tinsel hung. WE younger ones had to do it to suit him. One Christmas Eve, my Dad put on my red parka with a pointy hood over his head. He went outside with it on and pretended to be Santa Claus, saying, "Ho! Ho! Ho!" and "Merry Christmas!" How it delighted us! Christmas morning there were many gifts under the tree. We would have turkey dinner and mince meat tarts and home made chocolates and candies.

There was one Christmas that I remember so well. Times were tough and there wasn't much money to be had. We had a teeny little Christmas tree that sat on the washstand. In the morning, there were very few gifts. My treasured gift that year was a tin lunch kit—a black one that the lid flipped open and a place for a thermos to fit in the lid. I wasn't disappointed, though. I was tickled with my lunch box. It was new and shiny!

I have thought about that Christmas often over the years. I'm sure my parents felt bad that they couldn't buy us many gifts that year. They gave all they possibly could. We had a happy time—a time filled with love and laughter. We were thankful that we had a warm house and we had each other, and that was really all that mattered.

I wonder how thankful we are nowadays. We all have so much. Yet often we want more. We aren't satisfied with what we have. God gives and gives and gives. He gave us His only Son. He has given us health and family and jobs and homes. What have we done with it? Have we thanked Him for it?

Prayer Lord Jesus, help us to remember what all You have done for us. You give us the very breath that we breathe. You have given us everything. At this Christmas season, help us to focus on what is important, and that is You. You willingly sent Your Son to earth for us. Thank You. Amen

My Thoughts

Clean and Shiny

Matthew 11:29 Let me teach you, because I am humble and gentle, and you will find rest for your souls. (NLT)

One day I was pealing an onion. This must have been a very strong onion, because tears were just streaming down my face. Always when I am pealing an onion, I wonder why I am doing so. It is _not_ fun, but the flavor in the food to which I add the onion is enhanced. It just adds that extra little "zip".

The outer skin of an onion is crusty and hard. After I take off the crusty part, I wash the onion and it is shiny and clean.

I thought of my life. So often, I am crusty and hard on the outside--because of resentment, bitterness, pride, fear, jealousy, envy, wanting revenge. When I see that crustiness in my life and call out to God, confessing my sin, He gladly comes and gently peals the crusty layer off. He then washes me clean – just like I do with the onions.

Then, and only then, can I be white and shiny—on both the outside and the inside. My life can then flavor others' lives. Who knows the effect of a shiny, clean life?

Let's ever be conscious of the onion. Are we crusty and hard on the outside? Others don't see Jesus in us when we are like that. Or are we clean and shiny, bringing love, acceptance, and gentleness to others? I'm sure we all want to be shiny and bringing glory to God.

John 15:3 Now ye are clean through the word which I have spoken to you. (KJV)

> _Prayer Father God, thank You for the onion and how you made it. Every time we look at an onion, help us to remember the crusty part of our lives that needs to be removed. Help us to come to You quickly for cleansing. We claim the promise that You make us clean. Amen_

My Thoughts

Cleaning The Inside

Romans 8:29-30 For those whom He foreknew, He also predestined to become conformed to the image of His Son, so that He would be the firstborn among many brethren; and these whom He predestined, He also called; and these whom He called, He also justified; and these whom He justified, He also glorified. (NASB)

As I was cleaning out a pumpkin to make a jack-o-lantern, I realized how much we are like these pumpkins. I looked over the whole bin of pumpkins, and choose the one that I wanted. God also chooses us.

When the time came, I cut the top off the pumpkin. I looked inside and saw seeds that were not needed for the purpose I choose the pumpkin in the first place. I cleaned all the seeds out and threw them away. God looks inside us as well—into our hearts. He wants to take out all the unnecessary things in our lives--all the dependencies, all the addictions, all the seeds of sin.

1 John 1:9 If we confess our sins, He is faithful and just to forgive us our sins and to cleanse us from all unrighteousness. (KJV)

After I had all the seeds cleaned out, I cut holes for eyes, nose and mouth. I put a smiling face on him. I thought this is like us as well--once Jesus Christ has cleansed us of our sins, we are happy and rejoicing in the Lord.

Then I put a light in the jack-o-lantern. You notice its name has changed. At the beginning it was a pumpkin. Now it is a jack-o-lantern. Our name also changes once Jesus has come in.

Isaiah 62:2 You'll get a brand-new name straight from the mouth of GOD. (MSG)

The light shone brightly through the facial features I had made. So like us—Jesus' light shines through us—through our faces, through our smiling mouth, through our twinkling eyes. He has cleaned us—from the inside out. Praise God!

Prayer   Lord Jesus, help us remember that You have cleansed us. Help us to keep looking to You for continual cleansing that we so desperately need. Thank You for the power in Your blood to cleanse us. Amen

My Thoughts

Comfortable

1 John 1:9 On the other hand, if we admit our sins--make a clean breast of them--he won't let us down; he'll be true to himself. He'll forgive our sins and purge us of all wrongdoing. (MSG)

Years ago, I had a pair of shoes that lasted for years and years. The day finally came when I had to do something with them. I hated to do it too—they were so comfortable. My feet never hurt in them at all. I could be on my feet all day long in them, and it never bothered me. They were worn out, though, and not suitable to wear, even at home in the garden anymore. I had to make a choice to throw them away.

Character defects are something in our lives that we are comfortable with, things like pride, fear, anger, people pleasing, self-centeredness, and resentment. These things are hard to see in our lives. They usually have a long root. The root keeps producing fruit.

As hard as they are for us to see, we can ask God to show us our character defects. Then when He does, we can confess them and ask Him to remove them from us. And He will. He will transform us. It is a choice as well.

Romans 12:1-2 Offer yourselves as a living sacrifice to God, dedicated to His service and pleasing to Him . . . Let God transform you inwardly by a complete change of your mind. (GNB)

We want to please God with our lives. When the Holy Spirit convicts of us our sin, let's willingly and quickly confess it to Him. Let's offer ourselves to God. He will change us from the inside out.

Prayer Thank You, God, for your willingness and power to forgive us of our sin. Please show us every area in our lives that isn't pleasing to You. Help us, give us Your grace to look at those areas honestly and to run to You with them. Help us to claim the forgiveness that You so willing grant us. And help us to trust You to change us inwardly. Thank You. Amen

My Thoughts

Comparisons

Romans 8:1 Therefore there is now no condemnation for those who are in Christ Jesus. (NASB)

As a child, I was often compared to my siblings. Of course, I never measured up to the rest. It hurt. It caused me to withdraw, to condemn myself, to feel insecure, to feel worthless.

I carried that with me for years. Finally, someone helped me to see that I do have value. To establish that fact, I had to break the lies that I believed. In order to break the lies, I had to know the truth from the Word of God.

Condemnation was a strong hold in my life. The root had to be torn up by the truth.

More truths: *John 15:16* You did not choose Me, but I chose you. Jesus Christ chose me. He adopted me. *Ephesians 1:5* Because He is the King of kings, I am a princess! I do have value. *Colossians 2:10* In Him you have been made complete. Truth after truth sunk into my soul as I claimed them as mine.

May we ever look to Jesus Christ to know the truth about ourselves and not accept the lies that are tossed at us.

Prayer Father God, help us to deflect the negative words that are said to us, and often destroy our sense of self. Help us to search the Scriptures, and claim the truths about us from Your Word. Thank You. Amen

---

My Thoughts

Crumpled and Made Whole

Hosea 6:1 Come let us return to the Lord. For He has torn us, but He will heal us; He has wounded us, but He will bandage us. (NASB)

One day, my friend and I were installing curtains at church. She brought teeny little nails and a hammer to use. Because the wood was so hard, quite a few of those teeny nails bent over and crumpled under the pressure of the hammer.

I thought that was so much like us. So many times, we crumple under the stresses and pressures of life. We can't carry on any longer and we "fold".

The rest of the nails were strong and stood straight and true and were useful. Some of the bent nails were able to be straightened and were useful as well.

Life is full of pressure. Sometimes we crumple and think there is no use. Sometimes we stand up straight under the pressure. Sometimes we crumple at first but then "get straightened" by the Master and are useful again. He is a God of second chances, and third chances, and fourth chances, and so on. He will bandage us and will revive us. The key to that is in today's Scripture. Let us return to the Lord. That is the secret.

> _Prayer Father in Heaven, Thank You for Your promise that You will heal us, You will bandage us. Under the pressures of life and the crumpling experiences of life, help us to remember to come to You, for healing and wholeness. That is the only place it can happen. Thank You. Amen_

My Thoughts

Dandelions

1 John 1:9 If we confess our sins, He is faithful and righteous to forgive us our sins and to cleanse us from all unrighteousness. (NASB)

Aren't dandelions a bright pretty flower in the spring time? They tell us that spring has arrived. Children love bringing bouquets of them to their mothers, and mothers are delighted with the thoughtfulness of their children.

If left unattended, though, dandelions can cover the whole lawn and spread very quickly through out the neighborhood with their thousands of blown seeds. Our neighbor attacked her dandelion problem. Rather than use chemicals, she chose to dig out each root. Morning and night, she was out there digging and digging. It took her most of the summer to complete her task. The next spring, there were no dandelions to be seen in her yard. It was beautiful.

That was several years ago. This year, I noticed quite a few dandelions in her lawn again. She will have to dig them all out again.

In our lives, sometimes sin creeps in—like the dandelions in our yards. If left unattended, sin spreads—like the dandelions. God is so willing to forgive us and get rid of the sin, if only we will confess our sin to Him. Will we sin again? Of course! Every time God reveals sin in our hearts to us, He is waiting to forgive us and cleanse us, to get rid of that sin. It is a life long process—just like my neighbor digging the dandelions from her lawn.

Prayer Lord Jesus, please reveal to us the things in our hearts that make You sad. We do indeed want our hearts to be cleansed. Thank You for the power in Your blood to forgive and cleanse us. Amen

---

My Thoughts

Delight

<u>*Psalms 1:2*</u> But his delight is in the law of the LORD, And in His law he meditates day and night. (NASB)

<u>*Psalms 119:16*</u> I shall delight in Your statues; I shall not forget Your words. (NASB)

Easter was a special time of year in our family when I was a child. We would drive to the city on Good Friday and on Easter Sunday to attend church in our new Easter dresses and hats. Going to the city alone was exciting. Being in a big church was exciting. Wearing my new dress that Mom had made me was exciting. It was just a very memorable time of year.

Often when I went to bed at night, excited to be going to the city the next day, my new dress that Mom was making wasn't always completed. I would go to sleep with dreams of what it would be like in the morning. When I jumped out of bed in the morning, I would look until I found my dress, which was nicely pressed, ready for me to wear. I delighted in my new dress.

Always on Easter Sunday, we would sing "Christ Arose" by Robert Lowry. I loved the lyrics.
"Up from the grave He arose,
With a mighty triumph o'er His foes;
He arose a victor from the dark domain,
And He lives forever with His saints to reign;
He arose! He arose! Hallelujah! Christ arose!"

I delighted in the risen Savior!

Let's remember to delight in Jesus Christ, the risen Son of God, every day—not just at Easter time.

> *Prayer Father God, our hearts are filled with awe as we think of Jesus dying for us, going to hell for us, rising again for us. May we ever delight in Your finished work on the cross—for us. Thank You. Amen*

My Thoughts

Desires of our Hearts

Psalms 37:4-5 Delight yourself in the Lord; and He will give you the desires of your heart. Commit your way to the Lord, trust also in Him, and He will do it. (NASB)

Years ago when I was a child, my aunt told me about finding a twig on the street. She took the twig home, sanded it, cut it, varnished it, and made a beautiful necklace from it. She applied that to what Jesus does to us when He finds us and saves us. I thought it was so neat that she could find a spiritual lesson in such a simple thing.

As an adult, I met someone who could also see spiritual lessons in everything. I was amazed at her ability to do this.

I never consciously prayed about it; in fact, I never really thought much more about it. Looking back, I realize that God was working in my heart—even as a child. He put a desire in me to see spiritual lessons in every day events. I had to go on a bumpy road for quite a few years, though, in order to apply every day things to my spiritual life. Now, there isn't often a day that goes by that I don't see a spiritual application to something I experience or observe.

Even though I didn't know it at the time, I had the desire to grow and to see God in every situation, and to paint a word picture to share with others.

I give Him all the glory and honor for planting that seed so many years ago. My desire now is to use this gift to encourage and bless and strengthen others.

What desire has God put in our hearts? Maybe we aren't even aware of it yet. Let's be open to Him speaking to us and leading us one day at a time.

Prayer Lord Jesus, You know us better than we know ourselves. You have put desires in our hearts that we may not be aware of yet. You are faithful, and You will lead us on Your path if we are willing to listen and obey. Help us, O Lord. Amen

My Thoughts

Diligence

Psalms 199:4 Thou hast commanded us to keep thy precepts diligently. (KJV)

Ninety-nine percent of the time, I put on my make-up and do my hair before breakfast. One morning recently as I was getting ready to dash out the door to an appointment, I ran into the bathroom and put my lipstick on as usual. This time, though, I neglected to turn on the light. A block down the street, I realized with horror that I hadn't put on the rest of my makeup! So my lips looked great, but the rest of my face was pale. I dashed back home and made myself more presentable to go out. I was negligent that morning. I should have been diligent, and made sure I was ready to go out the door.

In our lives, sometimes we're negligent. We neglect to read God's Word; we neglect to pray; we neglect to build relationships; we neglect to set healthy boundaries. That is when we pale. I would like to suggest that we need to dash back into God's Word and find Him there.

Proverbs 7:15 Therefore came I forth to meet thee, diligently to seek thy face, and I have found thee. (KJV)

Prayer Lord Jesus, we come to You today, realizing how negligent we are at times. It is so easy to get too busy to do the important things in life. It is so easy to let our boundaries slacken. But You want us to be diligent, to be self-controlled, and to seek Your face diligently. If we do this, You promise that we will find You. Please help us. Amen

---

My Thoughts

"Do Not Be Afraid"

2 Timothy 1:7 For God hath not given us the spirit of fear; but of power, and of love, and of a sound mind. (KJV)

Recently, fear was overwhelming me--fear of people's reactions; fear of rejection; fear of being hurt emotionally; fear of letting go of circumstances. Basically, it was all fear of the unknown.

I started reading a devotional guide at the beginning of January. I marveled at the messages God gave me that first week when I was struggling with fear.

Luke 1:37 Nothing, you see, is impossible with God." (MSG)

That was the message I heard, loudly and clearly, from God the first day. I realized that since He made our galaxy, and holds it all in place, He can help me. He can hold me together and the situations in my life. He can teach me and guide me. He can lift me up and encourage me. That gave me a little ray of hope.

Luke 2:10 But the angel said to them, "Do not be afraid; for behold, I bring you good news of great joy which will be for all the people; (NASB)

When I'm filled with fear, God tells me, "Don't be afraid. I bring you good news of great joy." That said to me, "Judy, trust Me. I still accept you, I forgive you, I will provide for you, I will comfort you. There is better stuff coming. It said to me that Jesus Christ is healing me, and I will be filled with joy. I repented of my lack of trust in my Savior, Who died for me and gave Himself for me. I asked for His help to remember that I can't change circumstances in and around me. I also asked for help to be strong and honest. I knew that God had not given me the spirit of fear, but has given me the spirit of power, love, and a sound mind. Oh, how I need Jesus.

We can all hear from God. His message is that He loves us; He cares for us; He is our comfort; He forgives us; He provides for us; He heals us; He is our peace and joy; He is our strength; He has not given us the spirit of fear, but of power, of love and of a sound mind.

> *Prayer Lord Jesus, so many times, fear creeps into our lives. We know in our heads that nothing is impossible with You. But it isn't always in our hearts. We don't claim that truth. Many times in the Scriptures, You tell us not to fear, and in so doing, You are telling us to trust You. Help us, we pray, for we are a needy people. Amen*

My Thoughts

Doing Good

Psalms 1:2   But his delight is in the law of the Lord, and on his law he meditates day and night. (NIV)

Once after a busy day at work, I hurriedly drove to the gym for my daily exercise. I noticed there weren't many cars around and thought it must be due to the time of day. As I climbed out of the car, the manager came to meet me saying that the gym was closed because they had had a break-in during the night. There were pieces of shattered glass in the carpet so it wasn't safe for anyone to exercise that day.

I jumped back in my car and went home. There were several things awaiting my attention. The thing I chose to do was read my Bible and journal. I needed that time alone with God. It always amazes me what comes out of the end of my pen when I journal. I could see that God had allowed that break-in at the gym. Going to exercise had been a good thing to do, but God had something better in mind. He wanted me to spend time with Him alone.

So many times in our lives, we have plans to do so many good things. They really are good things. They have eternal value. But sometimes God has a better plan for us and that could be just to spend time with Him. He wants us to be like Him rather than to do good works. We are to serve God but there are times when the most important thing to do is spend time with Him.

Psalm 84:10   Better is one day in your courts than a thousand elsewhere. (NIV)

> *Prayer Lord Jesus, so many times we have such good plans. But You want us to spend time with You. Help us to remember that daily. Amen*

My Thoughts

Eating the Right Food

1 Peter 2:2 As newborn babes, desire the sincere milk of the word, that ye may grow thereby: (KJV)

Years ago, we had a little bush right outside our living room window. We were delighted one spring to discover a little nest in the bush. Before long, there were a few little eggs in it. We watched daily, with great anticipation, for the little birds to hatch! The day finally arrived. They were so tiny and so dependent on their parents. Almost constantly, the adult birds were bringing food for them. They knew the right food and where to find it. My! Did they ever grow quickly! Before long, they had flown away and were able to find their own food.

Oh, how we need to be fed as Christians. As baby Christians, we are hungry for the Word. At times, though, we just can't find the right food. Sometimes, we choke on the food. What do we do? Where do we start? The Bible is a big book with a lot of strange names in it. We need an adult to show us what the best food is for us, and where to find it in the Bible. Then, as we grow, we can scout around in God's Word ourselves, and find more food for our souls.

Let's always be aware that our soul needs to be fed. God's Word is that necessary food. He says, "Learn of me" in Matthew 11:29. (KJV)

Prayer Father God, thank You for Your Word whereby we can be fed and satisfied, and we can grow. Help us to spend time learning of You. Amen

---

My Thoughts

Empty Gas Tank

<u>Ephesians 5:18</u> Drink the Spirit of God, huge draughts of him. (MSG)

With my job, I drive a lot. As a result, I have to fill up the gas tank often. It shows empty far sooner than I would like. But I do know that I have to fill it if I want to complete my job. I need gas to finish what I set out to do for the day.

In our lives, we have a gas tank too. And often, it shows empty as well. When it is empty, it shows itself by discouragement, exasperation, depression, busyness, overeating, contempt, withdrawal, defensiveness, criticism, exhaustion.

Where do we go to get our personal, individual gas tanks filled up? We also go to the gas pump—the spiritual one. There is only one in the world. And we can all use it at the same time. Isn't that amazing?

Jesus is waiting and willing and ready to fill us up. May we recognize the signs of running empty and go quickly to Him to get filled. Actually, we need to be filled daily, hourly. Jesus can do it if we go to Him for filling.

> *Prayer Lord Jesus, thank You that You can fill each one of us at the same time. You are omnipotent. Help us to come to You for filling every day, every hour, every minute. We need You. Amen*

My Thoughts

Exercise

1 Timothy 6:11-12 But you, Timothy, man of God: Run for your life from all this. Pursue a righteous life--a life of wonder, faith, love, steadiness, courtesy. Run hard and fast in the faith. Seize the eternal life, the life you were called to, the life you so fervently embraced in the presence of so many witnesses. (MSG)

Exercise! Often when we hear that word, we cringe, knowing it is hard work.

In the physical realm, I have determined to get into shape and lose weight a few times over the years. Getting started is the hardest part. Then sticking with it can be a challenge as well. I have done this in order to improve my health and appearance.

How about spiritual exercise? Does our spirit need to be exercised? I would like to suggest it does. That can also be a hard choice—one we procrastinate on. How do we exercise spiritually? By reading God's Word, by praying, by attending church regularly, by believing God's truths, by nurturing Christian friendships, by memorizing His Word, by confessing our sin and our need for Jesus to be Lord of our lives. Then, we will become more like Christ. Others will see Jesus in us. When we grow a little, we are content with the increased joy and peace and contentment—just like when we exercise physically, we are encouraged by the few pounds or inches we lose. Sticking with the spiritual exercise is hard as well. Both physical and spiritual exercises are important.

1 Corinthians 3:16 Do you not know that you are a temple of God and that the Spirit of God dwells in you? (NASB)

May we ever be conscious of keeping our bodies and spirits healthy.

> *Prayer* Thank You, Lord, for the bodies that You have given us. Help us to take care of them. You live in us and how grateful we are for that. Help us to take a deep, hard look at the reasons we eat too much. I ask for Your grace. We are a needy people. Amen

My Thoughts

Following

Revelation 22:13 I am Alpha and Omega, the beginning and the end, the first and the last. (KJVR)

We used to have two Sheltie dogs. We got the second one a year after the first one. Tramp, the younger one, would always follow Lady. Wherever she went, he was right behind her. I never thought much about it. I just assumed that he had adopted Lady as his mother, and all was well.

After having them for several years, we clued in that Tramp was blind. He couldn't jump up into a truck. He would always miss. He would run right in front of a quad's wheel. Lady would be on the other side of the quad. Much to our dismay, he got ran over once by the quad. The treads on the tire never hurt him—he just hopped on up and kept going. Maybe if he had been following Lady, he wouldn't have been run over.

You know, God knows the beginning to the end. He is the beginning and He is the end. He knows all the in between stuff as well. He is omniscient. He wants us to follow Him, just like Tramp followed Lady. He trusted her completely. And that is what Jesus wants us to do with Him as well. There are times when we don't follow Jesus, and we get run over by the treads of life. We can hop up, dust ourselves off and keep going—just like Tramp did. Let's remember Lady and Tramp as we go about our daily lives.

> _Prayer Lord Jesus, we know you want us to follow You. And yet there are times, we get side tracked. Please forgive us. Help us to keep our eyes on You. Amen_

My Thoughts

Following Jesus

Matthew 9:9 As Jesus went on from there, he saw a man named Matthew sitting at the tax collector's booth. "Follow me," he told him, and Matthew got up and followed him. (NIV)

When I go to the mall by myself, I have often come out, have to stop, and wonder where in the world the car is. Other times, I park in the parking lot at work, and at the end of the day, I have to look and look for my car. It is so frustrating. Sometimes I'm sure that someone has come and towed my car away. Or I finally spot it a few rows away, go running up to it, and discover it isn't mine at all – but one the same model and color as mine.

Now, on the other hand, when my husband and I go shopping together, he usually drives. We park and walk into the store, do our shopping, and come out. I trust that he knows where the car is. When he is with me, I don't even think about having to find it. I just follow along to where he leads me.

In this journey we call life, there are times when we trust our own instincts, get lost, and can't find our way. Sometimes, we think we see the way--like I think I see my car--only to find out it wasn't the right way. It is only when we trust our Master, our Leader, that we know we are on the right path. He sees it clearly. We just have to follow.

Prayer Lord Jesus, we are so short-sighted. Often, we only see in front of our noses, but You know the right path on which for us to go. You see the whole picture when we can't possibly see it. Help us to trust You completely in every area of our lives. Help us to follow You like Matthew did in days of old. That is what You want from us. Amen

---

My Thoughts

Forgiveness

1 John 1:9 If we confess our sins, he is faithful and just to forgive us our sins, and to cleanse us from all unrighteousness. (KJV)

As I reminisce about our children when they were young, I remember the days of muddy little feet tracking into the house. They had been having fun—in the sprinkler on a hot day, in the mud puddles, or having a water fight. I can't count the number of times I washed the floor after they tracked into the house. It was easy to do—just get out the scrub bucket and mop. Before long, all was clean again.

We track on the floor of our lives too. Those tracks could be our trampling on a relationship, or living in denial that affects every aspect of our lives. They could be sneering at authority. The list can go on and on.

God sees the messes we make—the tracks on the floor of our lives. He is so willing to cleanse us and to get rid of the tracks, if only we will confess to Him--as our text for today says.

Prayer Lord Jesus, You see all the tracks we make. They don't surprise You at all, because You are omniscient. Thank You for the power in the blood of the Lamb to wash the tracks away, and give us a clean new start. Amen

---

My Thoughts

Fragrance of Jesus

2 Corinthians 2:15 Our lives are a fragrance presented by Christ to God. (NLT)

In our ladies' small group, we are learning to say a simple "Thank you" when someone compliments us. Most people try to minimize a compliment, so this is a learning process.

We also give each group member a hug when we leave. Last week, one lady hugged me and said, "You always smell so good!" to which I replied, "Thank you."

Our lives are to be fragrant. They are to be filled with Jesus Christ's fragrance—a sweet smell to those around us.

2 Corinthians 2:16 To those who are being saved, we are a life-giving perfume. (NLT)

I thought about the things in our lives that would prevent His fragrance from flowing through us. We could be burdened with work, ambition, hobbies, and sports. We could fill our lives with meaningless activity, with busyness, or addictions. We could be resentful, bitter, or badly hurt.

When these things are in our lives, Jesus' fragrance may be prevented from flowing through us. We need to spend time with Him daily, allowing Him to remove what needs to be removed, and allowing Him to spray His sweet fragrance into our hearts so others can smell His fragrance in us as we pass by.

2 Timothy 2:15 Study to shew thyself approved unto God, a workman that needeth not to be ashamed, rightly dividing the word of truth. (KJV)

Prayer Lord Jesus, our hearts yearn to be filled with Your fragrance. Yet too often, they are filled with rotten things. Please reveal those to us, and spray Your sweet fragrance deep into our hearts. We want others to perceive Your scent in our lives. Amen

---

My Thoughts

Freedom

Galatians 5:1   Christ has set us free to live a free life. So take your stand! Never again let anyone put a harness of slavery on you. (MSG)

Years ago, we had a budgie bird in our home. It was so tame. When out of its cage, it would follow us and sit on our shoulder. It would even land on the arm of our glasses and view the room from its lofty perch.

For some reason, one day the screen was out of the window and BJ flew away to what he thought was freedom. It was a windy day. Of course, the wind caught him and whipped him away. We never saw him again. He probably was wishing to come back to the security of his cage and the security of a home. But it was too late. Who knows what happened to BJ but I'm sure it wasn't good.

Christ has guidelines for us to follow. Sometimes it seems too confined, too small of walls. And yet, that is where we find our freedom.

Let's remember BJ when we are thinking of flying away on our own to do our own thing. Let's also remember that Christ set us free—free to choose His way in our lives.

Joshua 24:15 Choose you this day whom ye will serve; (KJVR)

Galatians 3:24 The law was like those Greek tutors, with which you are familiar, who escort children to school and protect them from danger or distraction, making sure the children will really get to the place they set out for. (MSG)

Prayer Jesus, thank You that You came to set us fee. Often we think we are bound by rule and regulations and laws. But those laws are in place to point us to Christ. Thank You. Amen

---

My Thoughts

Frowns

Philippians 4:4 Rejoice in the Lord always; again I will say, rejoice! (NASB)

1 Thessalonians 5:18 Thank God no matter what happens. This is the way God wants you who belong to Christ Jesus to live. (MSG)

Years ago, I caught myself frowning a lot. I would look in the mirror and see the lines in my forehead. It was an eye opener. I didn't want those creases to become permanent.

I thought about how easy it would be if I could just plug in the iron, turn it on and iron the wrinkles out. I knew I couldn't do that so had to make a choice. I could choose to carry the weight of the world on my shoulders and continue to frown or I could choose to praise God for His goodness to me and relax my facial muscles.

I'm happy to say at that time, I made the decision to rejoice in the Lord, and to be thankful for what God had given me. There are times, though, that I still pick up the load and carry it again—and yes, it does affect my facial expressions.

May we ever be conscious of the choices we make. Even in the midst of trouble, we can rejoice.

James 1:2 Consider it all joy, my brethren, when you encounter various trials. (NASB)

We can rejoice because God is good; we can rejoice because He knows what is best for us; we can rejoice because we are growing and becoming more like Him.

> *Prayer Thank You, Lord, that we do have choices. You have made us that way. We can choose to love You or not. We can choose to be thankful or not. We can choose to rejoice in You or not. Help us to always make the right choice. Amen*

My Thoughts

God Cares

1 Peter 5:7 God cares for you, so turn all your worries over to him. (CEV)

Years ago, when I was struggling with live in many areas, I would give those issues to God. I am a visual person so needed something that I could see that was meaningful to me. Someone suggested that I draw a conveyor belt, and then draw the problems on the conveyor belt, going up to God in heaven, pictured by a cloud. I did that many times over the years. For me, it sure did help to see it.

More recently, when I struggle with specific issues in my life, I have been visualizing and drawing an arrow, flying up to God with my issue on it. I think I like this second visual better. Arrows go much faster than conveyor belts. I like it because it seems to reach God quicker than on a conveyor belt. I can see it flying through the air to God, because I know He cares for me.

Some may not have to visualize or draw the picture of giving their problems to God. The main thing is that we do give our struggles to God. Sometimes, the thing we have to give to God is ourselves. I have often drawn myself on that conveyor belt or arrow.

Romans 12:1-2 Dear friends, God is good. So I beg you to offer your bodies to him as a living sacrifice, pure and pleasing. That's the most sensible way to serve God. Don't be like the people of this world, but let God change the way you think. Then you will know how to do everything that is good and pleasing to him. (CEV)

Let's give God ourselves so that we will know how to do everything that is good and pleasing to God. Let's not carry our own troubles but rather give them to the Lord. He promises to carry them for us.

Psalm 55:22 Pile your troubles on GOD's shoulders-- he'll carry your load, he'll help you out. He'll never let good people topple into ruin. (MSG)

> _Prayer Lord Jesus, how our hearts thrill to know You care so much for us. We claim these truths as ours today. Thank You. Amen_

My Thoughts

Grace

2 Corinthians 12:9 And He has said to me, "My grace is sufficient for you, for power is perfected in weakness." (NASB)

Acts 5:29 Then Peter and the other apostles answered and said, We ought to obey God rather than men. (KJVR)

A few years ago, I had a falling out with some people whom I loved and who had supported me through the years. There were many misunderstandings. Most of these people, I had not seen for a very long time.

Recently, most of them were at a conference which I was attending. The messages given during the conference were very powerful. In the morning, God impressed on my heart that I should go and hug these people. I argued with God for a while about it. I was filled with fear—fear of their reactions, fear of judgement, fear of rejection. God reminded me that He has "not given me the spirit of fear, but has given me the spirit of love and power." (2 Timothy 1:7 KJV) God did win out. He assured me of His promise in our text for today: His grace is sufficient. As soon as lunch break came, I made my way quickly to find them. With no explanation, I hugged each one of them. It helped to heal my heart even more.

Let's always keep in mind that whatever God asks us to do, He will give us the grace to do it. Fear does not come from God. He gives us the spirit of love and power. Let's obey God—rather than listening to our fears.

> *Prayer   Thank You, Jesus, for Your grace that is bountiful and it is sufficient to meet our every need. Help us to claim that truth as ours. Amen*

My Thoughts

Grace When Needed

Hebrews 4:16 Let us have confidence, then, and approach God's throne, where there is grace. There we will receive mercy and find grace to help us just when we need it. (GNB)

I have colored my hair myself for years. I would go to the store and pick a color that I thought was closest to my natural hair color.

Then, I decided that I would go to a salon and have it professionally colored. That way, it would always be the same color when it was finished. However, the expense of doing this is an issue, so one day, I decided I would color my own hair once again. I dashed to the drug store, chose a color and brought it home, excited to be saving money.

When the coloring process was done, and I washed and crème rinsed it, I was horrified at the color of my hair. It was almost black. I panicked and ran to the store again to buy a lighter color, hoping it would lighten my hair. It didn't.

This was early on Friday evening. I knew my hair stylist's shop was open late on Fridays, so I called her to see if I could get in and if she could do something with my hair. The timing was wonderful. She had a cancellation. So in I went. She streaked it, and it looked really good when she was finished. She never charged me for that appointment, under one condition: that I would never color my hair by myself again.

I had created the problem of the color of my hair by a choice. I looked at myself in the mirror and saw what mistake I had made. I called my stylist. She treated me with grace—even though I did not expect that at all. What more could I want?

2 Corinthians 9:8 And God is able to make all grace abound to you, so that having all sufficiency in all things at all times, you may abound in every good work. (ESV)

So many times, we cause problems in our own lives by choices we make. Sometimes, we don't know how we got there. Often, we can see the results of our choices though. We do have an avenue to follow during these times. We can call on God. And He treats us with grace. Isn't that wonderful?

> *Prayer God, thank You so much for your grace extended to us. We can't do life on our own. We need Your grace every minute of every day. Help us to look at ourselves and reach out to You. Amen*

My Thoughts

Grieving the Holy Spirit

Ephesians 4:30-32 Do not grieve the Holy Spirit of God, by whom you were sealed for the day of redemption. Let all bitterness and wrath and anger and clamor and slander be put away from you, along with all malice. Be kind to one another, tender-hearted, forgiving each other, just as God in Christ also has forgiven you. (NASB)

This summer a rock was thrown into the window at the gym where I work out. It was no little rock. It was huge. The whole big window was smashed into tiny splinters all over the carpet. The damage was phenomenal. The owner and manager were grieved by this act of violence by someone who never thought about the damage they were doing. It took time to repair the window so the gym was useable again.

I thought about the words that are sometimes carelessly thrown from our mouths—most often directed at our loved ones. Most times, we don't think about the damage our words do to those we love the most. But they crash; they smash; they splinter. Oh, how it grieves the Holy Spirit when we treat each other in such hurtful ways. God is ready and willing to help us with our words if only we ask Him.

Psalms 141:3 Post a guard at my mouth, GOD, set a watch at the door of my lips. (MSG)

> *Prayer Lord Jesus, so many times we say such hurtful things. Not only do we hurt the ones to whom we speak, but we also hurt You, because You are a God of relationships. When we do damage with our words, we break relationships and that grieves You. Please post a guard at our mouths, God, and set a watch at the door of our lips. We give You the honor and glory and praise. Amen*

My Thoughts

Growing

<u>Philippians 1:6</u> For I am confident of this very thing, that He who began a good work in you will perfect it until the day of Christ Jesus. (NASB)

As another school year has started, I have been reminiscing about my school years and those of my children. How exciting it was to go back to school the first day of September.

As a child, I would always have a new outfit to wear to school the first day. I remember my mother finishing up a new dress after I went to bed. Oh, the excitement of getting up in the morning, and seeing my new dress hanging there, ready to wear to school. How I would dance around in my new dress. Mom would look on with glee, and be proud of her accomplishment.

Then, of course, there were shoes to buy. Often, my old ones would be way too small and even hurting my feet a little bit. That was because I was growing, and that was good and normal. Every year, I grew a bit taller, and looked a bit more like my mother.

It is also good and normal for us to grow as Christians and become more like Jesus. Yes, sometimes, it hurts—just like my old shoes. Hurts can come in many forms—emotional such as rejection, judgment, harsh words spoken to us. Hurts can be financial and we don't know where our next dollar is coming from. Hurts can be physical—a pain, a sickness, a disease. God knows which hurt fits us in order to make us grow. Oh, may we learn to trust Him during the hurting times in our lives. Bit by bit, we do grow and have a new wardrobe—one that pleases Jesus more every year.

> *Prayer Jesus, we don't like hurting, but we do want to grow. It seems that often the two go together. Help us to have an eternal view when life hurts, knowing that You are looking on, and are pleased that we are growing to become like You. Thank You. Amen*

My Thoughts

Growth

<u>1 Peter 2:2-3</u> You must crave pure spiritual milk so that you can grow into the fullness of your salvation. Cry out for this nourishment as a baby cries for milk, now that you have had a taste of the Lord's kindness. (NLT)

In years gone by, I have started plants in early spring in the house. I used the peat pots that are compressed. They were all the same size and shape when I took them out of the package – all fifty of them. They were all uniform, and had no individuality at all. You just add water to them, and within minutes, they had grown. I could almost see them grow. Shortly, some were struggling to grow; some had already reached the maximum height; some were in between. It was so interesting.   I noticed that some had a steady supply of water, and the others didn't.

As I was sitting there and watching them, I thought about us as Christians. As newborn babes in Christ, we are all the same size at first. We start out brand new babies, needing the milk of the Word. I have noticed over the years that some people, who have been Christians for a very long time, still need the milk of the Word. Then, there are others, who have been Christians only for a short time, who are eating meat. Why the difference? I think, in part, the reason is that some of us are just so hungry for the Word, we devour as much milk as we possibly can. In so doing, we grow faster and become more mature more quickly. The supply of the milk is in the Word of God. We are being saturated with God's Word like the peat pots were with water.

> *Prayer Lord Jesus, thank you for your Word. The way to the fullness of your salvation is by reading it, and applying it to our lives. We cry out for that nourishment. We do want to grow. Help us to spend time learning more about you. Amen*

My Thoughts

Harmony or Discord?

<u>Psalms 143:10</u> Teach me to do your will, for you are my God; may your good Spirit lead me on level ground. (NIV)

I have often sat enthralled watching a band play. All those instruments going at the same time and the wonderful music that comes out of it thrills me. The beautiful music soothes my soul. It is wonderful harmony.

In our church, we have a full band playing at all times. It is wonderful. Recently, I have been learning to play the synthesizer as part of this band. I don't have any one-on-one time with a musician to learn what I am supposed to be doing. During practice, the pianist says to do this or that. I try desperately to do as she suggests. So many times, I hit the wrong note, I hit the wrong chord, I do the timing wrong. The discord that comes from that one little instrument is horrible. There are rules and guide lines in playing any instrument. As the months go by, I am learning more of those rules and the harmony that comes from that same little instrument is wonderful. The pianist is so patient and understanding.

I thought about our lives one day in reference to a band. We can live our lives in harmony or in discord. We can choose to stick to the rules and guidelines that God gives us in His word or we can choose to do our own thing. We can choose to learn or not to learn. It takes time for all of us to learn so that harmony can come out of our lives. That is what God wants. Yes, often, we hit the wrong chord, we hit the wrong note, we do the timing wrong but God is patient and merciful and will help us hit the right chord, the right note, do the right timing. He understands our frailty.

> *Prayer   Lord Jesus, thank You that you understand my failings. So many times, I see discord coming from my life and yet, You are patient with me. Please continue to work in my life so that I can see harmony flowing out of my life. It is ALL from You. Help me to learn the rules and guidelines that You have in place for me. I love you. Amen*

My Thoughts

Health

2 Timothy 2:15 Study to show thyself approved unto God, a workman that needeth not to be ashamed, rightly dividing the word of truth. (KJVR)

For years, I struggled with migraine headaches. I did discover a couple of the triggers, so I tried to avoid them to the best of my ability. Unfortunately, it wasn't always possible.

Then, I found a product that was said to boost my health in every way. I never thought about it helping my migraines. I just wanted to feel better all around. After several months of taking it, I realized that, yes, I did feel better physically—but also, that I hadn't had a migraine since having started taking it. Taking this product is now a priority in my life.

I have likened this experience to taking the Word of God into our souls every day. If we continually read His Word, and apply it to our lives, we are healthier spiritually, emotionally, and often physically. Sometimes, by reading God's Word, one area of our lives improves, and that affects the whole.

Let us put spending time with God as a priority in our lives. Our souls need to be fed, and we do that by reading His Word, praying, and communicating with Him. Often, journaling is helpful as well. Time hearing the message of God's servants is beneficial. Small group life is important. We need each other to help us along the path of life.

Prayer Thank You, Lord Jesus, for Your written Word that You have given us. Help us to really know in our hearts that there is power in Your Word to keep us healthy, for then, and only then, will we set our time with You as a priority. Amen

My Thoughts

Healthy No's

Proverbs 20:25 An impulsive vow is a trap; later you'll wish you could get out of it. (MSG)

When our children were little, I would often tell them "No". They would want to go play in the mud puddles. After I told them "No", I realized, I didn't mean it at all. It is fun to play in mud puddles. I didn't care if they got all wet and muddy. That is part of the fun. It was confusing for them. After I realized what I was doing, I was more conscious of my decisions.

Then there were times in my life when I would agree to do something for someone, and later resent it because I really didn't want to. Often, time was an issue, or I just didn't want to. I just couldn't say "No". I was afraid to say "No". I wanted their approval. I thought I was being spiritual by helping everyone who asked. I thought I was pleasing God.

I am not such a people pleaser anymore, and I know being involved with everything isn't necessarily spiritual. I have learned to say "No" at appropriate times.

I think so often we jump on ahead of God's timing because someone asked us to do something. It may not necessarily be in God's plan for our lives right now. We need to wait for His leading, His timing, His "Yes" or "No".

Habakkuk 2:3 These things I plan won't happen right away. Slowly, steadily, surely the time approaches when the vision will be fulfilled. If it seems slow, wait patiently for it will surely take place. It will not be delayed. (NLT)

> _Prayer Lord Jesus, we do want to serve You. We want to be pleasing to You. We long to be a blessing to others. But there are times, Lord, when we want to please people more than we want to please You. We want their approval. That approval is here and now. It is far more important to have Your approval. Help us to hear Your voice, and do only the things that You want us to do. We may not hear approval from others, but that is okay. Deep in our hearts, we know we have followed You, and that is what counts. Thank You for living in us. Amen_

My Thoughts

Heat

Job 23:10 But He knows the way I take; When He has tried me, I shall come forth as gold. (NASB)

Recently, I went to the cupboard to find a muffin to eat. I had baked them a few days prior. Oh my, was it ever dry! I immediately stuck it in the microwave, and it was nice and hot, with much-improved flavor and texture.

When we bake, we add ingredients, we stir, we mix, and we put it into a pan. Then we stick it in the oven (in the heat) in order to finish the process. After awhile, though, it does dry out. That is when the microwave comes in handy. We pop it into the microwave for a few seconds, and it is almost like new. More heat has been applied to make it soft and warm, and often edible.

Aren't stoves and microwaves wonderful? Stoves cook our meat, potatoes, and vegetables. In olden days, they would provide the heat for the home. They bake our bread, cakes, cookies and pies. Microwaves thaw out frozen food. They warm up food. They are amazing. How did we ever live without them? To perform these tasks, heat is required.

The older I'm getting, the more I am realizing that to produce a finished product, we need heat in our lives as well. At times, we dry out a bit, so some more heat is applied to soften and warm us up a bit. Oh, how we resist the heat of tribulation, though! Our flesh doesn't like it. It is painful. Heat burns. But—look at the finished product! What do we see? If we look closely, we can see us coming forth as gold--as in our text today. It is a process. It takes time.

Zechariah 13:8b-9 A third will be left in the land. I will bring that group through the fire and make them pure, just as gold and silver are refined and purified by fire. They will call on my name, and I will answer them. I will say, "These are my people," and they will say, "The Lord is our God." (NLT)

> *Prayer Lord Jesus, we do need heat in our physical daily lives to survive--heat from the sun, heat from the furnace in our long, cold winter months, a mother's warmth. Yet we resist heat to shape us and mold us to become more like You. Help us to trust You—especially in the heated times of our lives. Amen*

My Thoughts

Heated Times

Hebrews 13:5 He himself has said, "I WILL NEVER DESERT YOU, NOR WILL I EVER FORSAKE YOU," (NASB)

I remember well watching the clock as a child. The times I remember the most are when Mom was baking cookies or a cake. Oh, the aroma coming from the oven! It seemed like an eternity before the cookies were out of the oven. Of course, they were, then, too hot to eat. After they were taken off the cookie sheet, I still had to wait longer for them to cool. How I wish I could have sped up the process. The truth is, that if I could have, the cookies would not have been baked completely. They would have still been a bit raw, a bit doughy, and maybe a bit harsh.

We all go through a baking process in our lives. Each one of our baking processes is different. Some of us go through financial stress, or relational stress, or emotional stress, or health issues. I think all these things are a baking time. When we are going through those times, how we wish we could speed it up. If we were able to do so, then I am afraid the finished product would not be the same. We would not be baked completely. We would be a bit raw, a bit doughy, a bit harsh maybe. It could frustrate God's work of grace in our lives. It could certainly harm the process, not help it.

John 12:25 In the same way, anyone who holds on to life just as it is destroys that life. But if you let it go, reckless in your love, you'll have it forever, real and eternal. (MSG)

Let's surrender to those baking times in our lives. Let's be willing to stay in the oven as long as we need to be. We know that God is with us even during those heated times in our lives.

> *Prayer Lord Jesus, baking times are hard for us. Those times in the oven seem to never end. The time seems like it is going to go on forever. We cry out to You today to give us the endurance we need, the faith we need, the strength we need to go through the heat. Thank You that You will never leave us nor forsake us. Help us to cling to Your truths. Amen*

My Thoughts

Hill Country

Joshua 17:18 But the hill country shall be yours. For though it is a forest, you shall clear it, and to its farthest borders it shall be yours; for you shall drive out the Canaanites, even though they have chariots of iron and though they are strong." (NASB)

I have been in the foothills of Alberta, Canada, quite a few times. When we drive through them, there are many hills to go up and down. It takes more gas than driving on our flat prairie. At times, we have taken a walk in the foothills. Then we especially notice the hills—exerting lots of energy climbing up, but also a different kind of energy bracing ourselves coming down the hills. It also takes a lot of faith to climb those hills—faith to know that we can make it, faith to know that we can put one foot ahead of the other, faith to know the top of the hill is there, even though, we cannot see it all the time.

As we age, we aren't always able to climb hills. We sit and watch the younger generation tackle that adventure with enthusiasm. We can enjoy watching them, and pray for them as they climb the hills.

In our young years, we are strong and carry on climbing with faith in God, trusting Him to get us to the top of the hill. Then, the next generation comes along. We don't have the energy to keep up any more. We do have the power to pray, though. What a huge responsibility that is. What a connection with God. It also draws us closer to people. We can drive out the enemy by praying. Praying is one form of being a warrior for the Lord. May we ever be conscious of this truth.

Prayer Lord, sometimes, when we get a bit older, we feel pretty useless. We aren't needed as much. We can't keep up with the fast pace of life. But, Jesus, we know there is a purpose for us here, or You would have taken us home to be with You. Sometimes, we think that praying is such a minimal, insignificant part of life. Please remove that thinking pattern from us. We can tread down enemies by prayer. It is all because of Your power. We give You the honor and glory. Thank You for laying it on our hearts to pray—for those in need, for safety, for comfort, for strength, for peace, for healing, for fulfillment, that is only found in You. We love You, Lord. Amen

My Thoughts

Hope

<u>2 Timothy 1:7</u> For God gave us not a spirit of fearfulness; but of power and love and discipline. (ASV)

I have changed jobs a few times over the years. In each case, there is some reason I chose to resign from that position. The older I get, the harder I find the interviews for a new job. And yet, at the same time, I know I can't stay at my old job. The hope of a new job, which I would like better or which would have better work conditions is what spurs me on and helps me through those tough interviews. I find that change is also more difficult as I grow older. Adjusting to a new boss, new co-workers, and new responsibilities is progressively harder as well. But there is always the hope of something better.

In our lives, we go through changes. We go through hard times. Sometimes we get stuck in an old habit, an old hang-up. Then, we see a ray of hope somewhere. It could be that we see a change in someone else's life, and we inquire what worked for them. It could be counseling, or a recovery program, or a number of things. With that little ray of hope, we pursue something that will help us. It is hard at times. We face issues in our lives that we don't necessarily want to look at. And yet, the hope that things will improve is what encourages us to keep on. It may take a short time or a long time, but the light at the end of the tunnel begins to grow bigger and bigger. Our hope increases, and eventually, we have come out into the sunlight once again.

Sometimes, our habits and hang-ups are very comfortable. We don't always like change in those areas, and yet, we know that we are stuck. Change is a good thing—even though the unknown is scary. Let's not shy from working through the hard things in our lives. Let's step through the fear and pursue the hope that God has given us.

<u>Psalms 31:24</u> Be strong, be courageous, all you that hope in the LORD. (GNB)

> *Prayer   Lord Jesus, we come to You filled with fear—fear of the unknown, fear of changing, even fear of staying where we are. And yet, we know that something is wrong in our hearts. Help us, we pray, to trust You, to take those steps to health. We cling to Your Word that You have given us the spirit of power and love and discipline. You tell us to be strong and courageous. Oh, how we need You today! Amen*

My Thoughts

Hot Griddles

Hebrews 12: 6 For the Lord disciplines those he loves, and he punishes those he accepts as his children. (NLT)

We love pancakes in our house. Along with bacon and eggs, they have always been a Sunday morning treat.

One day as I was flipping pancakes, I thought about our lives. Often we are on the "hot griddle" of life. God is looking down tenderly on us to see how we are doing. The "bubbles" of anger, resentment, pride, bitterness and hurt come up to the surface and pop. Sometimes those "bubbles" are directed at innocent people who just happen to be in the way at the moment. The bubbles don't all pop at the same time. Some take longer. Some are larger. Some are smaller. Out of necessity, though, they must pop.

Sometimes, we are on the "hot griddle" of life because we need some discipline from God. At times, that can make us angry, resentful and bitter as well. But God is still looking down on us tenderly, watching to see how we are doing—knowing that it is for our own good.

God watches carefully to see when all the "bubbles" are popped out of our lives. He tends to us lovingly, and when the time is right, He flips us over to "heal" the soft, tender, oozing side. That's when we swell and grow—knowing how much Jesus Christ loves us. We rise, rejoicing because He has healed us from the hurt and pain, or we are through the discipline that He sent our way.

Hebrews 12: 11 No discipline is enjoyable while it is happening—it is painful! But afterward there will be a quiet harvest of right living for those who are trained in this way. (NLT)

> *Prayer Lord Jesus, life is so painful at times. There are times we need to be disciplined. There are times painful things happen that we have no control over. But You are watching. You see what is happening. You know when we need discipline. Thank You for that. Help us to trust You enough to know that You are in control, and there will be a quiet harvest of right living later on. Amen*

My Thoughts

Insanity versus Sanity

James 1:21 So throw all spoiled virtue and cancerous evil in the garbage. In simple humility, let our gardener, God, landscape you with the Word, making a salvation-garden of your life. (MSG)

In the recovery program at our church, we emphasize the definition of insanity as doing the same thing over and over again but expecting different results. When I thought about it, I realized the truth of it. Reckless, careless drivers are stopped by policemen. They are given a ticket. The hope is that they will drive more carefully. Often, it doesn't happen. They continue driving recklessly, and they continue receiving tickets from the policemen. The drivers are expecting a different result—even though they continue being careless.

The pattern continues in our personal lives as well. Often, we lash out at others, and they respond in self-defense. Or our tone of voice is wrong, and we wonder why our relationships are deteriorating. Or we are too busy to spend time in God's Word and praying, and we just can't understand why our Lord and Savior isn't speaking to us anymore. We expect things to change, but they don't.

James 3:5 A word out of your mouth may seem of no account, but it can accomplish nearly anything--or destroy it! It only takes a spark, remember, to set off a forest fire. (MSG)

The dictionary definition of sanity is mental balance or health, sensibleness, reasonableness. Another way of saying that would be changing what we do so that the results would be different. If the reckless driver slowed down and drove sensibly, he wouldn't receive a ticket. If we spoke to others with respect, they wouldn't react negatively to us. If we spent time with God, He would speak to us.

Having health and mental balance includes looking at our past and present hurts, hang-ups and habits. Through that process, God can heal us. The results of our daily living will change—they will be different. Praise God!

Prayer Lord, we haven't seen that the definition of insanity is doing the same thing over and over again expecting a different result. Yet at times, we wonder why we are stuck where we are. Deep down in our hearts, we do want to change. We don't want to continue living the same old way we have for years. We want growth. We want to see a change in ourselves. We want to reflect You in our lives-at home as well as in public. How miserably we fail at times, though. Please forgive us. Help us every minute of every day to follow You in every decision. Fill us with Your grace, we pray. In Jesus' Name we pray. Amen

My Thoughts

Inspirations in the Key of "J"

Jeremiah 29:11 I know what I'm doing. I have it all planned out--plans to take care of you, not abandon you, plans to give you the future you hope for. (MSG)

I have been writing devotionals for a few years now. It all started rather innocently. I was subscribed to the Presbyterian Church in Canada's *Daily* devotional which I read every day. At the end of each devotional, there is a little blurp about praying about writing devotionals. That started my seeing spiritual lessons in everyday events. I wrote only a few at first and submitted them. As time went on, I kept writing and submitting others.

A few years ago, one of the readers from another country offered to publish a book of my devotionals. That was an exciting thought, but I never pursued it. I finally decided that I could self-publish right here in my own town in order to save the cost of freight. I prayed a lot about this and talked to my accountability partner about it. I decided to pursue it with a couple of local printers.

About ten months after beginning the process, the book, *Inspirations in the Key of "J"*, was completed. It included a piano music CD that I had made. That was also a lengthy process—times of waiting for others to do what I couldn't. But what joy to see and hold the book that I had penned, and had self-published! What a delight! What excitement! The joy of the Lord filled my heart!

Nehemiah 8:10 The joy of the LORD is your strength. (NASB)

In our lives, we often have a goal. Sometimes, it may get blocked by numerous obstacles. Often, there are problems that are beyond our control. We can be impatient, but the ultimate goal is for us to learn patience through these times. To cover these times in prayer is so beneficial.

Romans 5:3 There's more to come: We continue to shout our praise even when we're hemmed in with troubles, because we know how troubles can develop passionate patience in us. (MSG)

Prayer *Thank You, Lord Jesus, for giving us goals and dreams. How sweet it would be if the road were smooth to accomplish those goals and fulfill those dreams. So often, the enemy attacks during these times. Help us to look to You continually for strength and perseverance to continue on the path that You want us to go on. Bless us, we pray, as we seek to fulfill Your plans for us. We know that Your plan is to take care of us and to give us a future that we hope for. Thank You. Amen*

My Thoughts

Interior Cleanliness?

<u>Matthew 23:27</u> Woe unto you, scribes and Pharisees, hypocrites! For ye are like unto whited sepulchers, which indeed appear beautiful outward, but are within full of dead men's bones, and of all uncleanness. (KJV)

We have been doing some house renovations recently— both inside and outside. The outside is all done now, but the inside is just beginning. There is some dry wall work done, but a lot more to do. We are taking some walls out, and the mess is still ahead of us. From the outside of our house, it looks beautiful. When one little grandson drove up with his parents, he said, "Grandma has a new house!" Inside, though, it doesn't look very new.

My thoughts turned to people. Some of us look *really* good on the outside, but what is actually going on inside that no-one can see? Is it as clean and shiny on the inside? Do we have it all together like we portray?

Only God knows our hearts. Only He can clean up the inside, and that is only if we let Him. Let's open our hearts to Him, and let Him do the work in us that we so desperately need.

<u>Psalms 51:2</u> Wash me thoroughly from mine iniquity and cleanse me from my sin. (KJV)

Prayer Father in Heaven, we don't want to be hypocrites. We want to be clean and beautiful on the inside, as well as on the outside. Please reveal to us the "dead man's bones" inside us that we need to face. Help us not to deny them and put on a good exterior. We trust You, Jesus. Amen

---

My Thoughts

Invited In

John 3:16 "This is how much God loved the world: He gave his Son, his one and only Son. And this is why: so that no one need be destroyed; by believing in him, anyone can have a whole and lasing life." (MSG)

Revelation 3:20 "Look at me. I stand at the door. I knock. If you hear me call and open the door, I'll come right in and sit down to supper with you. (MSG)

Years ago, we stayed in a little cabin in Banff, Alberta, Canada, on our way to British Columbia to visit relatives. It was a neat little cabin with a few rooms in it. We thought we had locked the door before retiring. None of us checked it, though. We just presumed it was done. In the middle of the night, the door opened, and someone came into our cabin. As soon as he knew he was in the wrong cabin, he left hurriedly, likely embarrassed for intruding. We had not invited him in. He did not knock. He just came in.

We have a room, a cabin, if you will, in our lives as well. Someone is standing at the door knocking, waiting for us to say come in. We do know His Name -- it is Jesus. He wants to come in, and give us eternal life. All we have to do is open the door, and let Him in. At times, after Jesus is in our cabins, we don't want Him to dine with us. We stubbornly refuse to let Him sit down to have supper with us. We are missing out on so much. He wants that relationship with us.

Let's be sure that we have asked Jesus Christ to come in to dwell in our cabins. Once He is with us, let's remember to have supper with Him. May we ever let Him teach us, and guide us. May we ever learn from Him.

Psalms 46:10 Be still, and know that I am God. (KJVR)

> *Prayer   Lord Jesus, You are so patient, waiting while You are knocking on our heart's door. Thank you, God. Help us to be still so that we can know You are God. Teach us, we pray. Amen*

120

My Thoughts

Is God Trustworthy?

Hebrews 2:13   I will put my trust in him. (KJV)

2 Chronicles 20:15   Thus says the LORD to you, 'Do not fear or be dismayed because of this great multitude, for the battle is not yours but God's. (NASB)

At six months of age, my twin and I had to go live with two of our aunts (my twin at one place and I at another) for six months because Mom was hospitalized. Having two older children, Dad couldn't possibly take care of us twins, and do all the farming and housework, as well. Mom's cousin came to help out at home. My aunts did the best they could possibly do to provide safety and security for us. Mom told me years later that I wasn't happy at my aunt's house, but the minute I got home, I was content. Looking back and understanding more, I see that I felt abandoned by my family.

This feeling carried on into my adult years. When I went through rough times, I felt abandoned by God. I didn't know He was really trustworthy. I talked to my Dad about it once. He assured me that I could trust God. My pastor affirmed that truth. So I decided because my Dad and my pastor both said God is trustworthy, I would trust God.

Oh, how hard it was at first. God is faithful--and proved Himself trustworthy time after time to me. He showed me little by little, how I could trust Him. That battle was not mine to start with. I had to let go, and let God win the battle.

Are we struggling with questions and doubts about God's trustworthiness? Will we get through this dark tunnel? Let's trust His Word. We go through life little by little – step by step. Let's trust Him with all our heart, soul, and mind.

> *Prayer Thank you, Father God, for being faithful and trustworthy. People let us down, but You never will. Help us to keep our eyes on You—especially when we're full of doubts. Help us to continue to trust You also when things are going well. Amen*

My Thoughts

Jack-o'-Lantern

Philippians 1:6 There has never been the slightest doubt in my mind that the God who started this great work in you would keep at it and bring it to a flourishing finish on the very day Christ Jesus appears. (MSG)

As I was thinking about making a jack-o'-lantern, I realized that the poor pumpkin has to go through some pain in order to become a jack-o'-lantern. Yes, I know the pumpkin can't feel anything. Imagine with me, though, for a few minutes what it would be feeling, if it could.

I took the sharp knife and cut the top off. Can you imagine the pain? This is a crisis situation for the pumpkin. Then I scraped the seeds out – oh, scraping is painful--as well as being another crisis. Then I cut eyes, and nose, and mouth to make a smiling face. That would have hurt too. From the pumpkin's perspective, crises kept piling up and piling up. How the pumpkin would have been wailing and sobbing and crying in pain! Imagine how he must have felt--like he just couldn't bear any more. If he could talk, he probably would have pleaded for me to stop. But I just kept on cutting and shaping and molding to what I wanted. I did care about the pain he was in, but I also had a purpose in mind when I started. The pumpkin was just a pumpkin and had no idea what its purpose in life was. In the end, I stood back and was pleased with the smiling jack-o'-lantern.

We go through pain in our lives as well. Often, we face one crisis after another. Sometimes, we wail and sob and beg for the pain to stop. But there is a higher reason, a higher calling, a higher purpose for our lives. We go through struggles, pain, and crises because God, Who started the work in us, will keep at it until we see Him face to face. We will be as pure as gold. (Job 23:10)

Are we yielding to the pain or are we rebelling against the working of God in our hearts?

I love the song, *He's Still Workin' on Me*, by Joel Hemphill—

He's still workin' on me
To make me what I ought to be;
It took Him just a week
To make the moon and stars,
The sun and the earth
And Jupiter and Mars.
How loving and patient He must be!
He's still workin' on me.

Prayer Lord Jesus, we don't like crises; we don't like pain. But neither do we see the finished product of our lives. Help us to trust You during these times, because You say that You will keep working on us. We do appreciate that in the long run, but, oh, it is hard sometimes. Help us, we pray. Amen

My Thoughts

"Jet"

Philippians 4:8-9 Summing it all up, friends, I'd say you'll do best by filling your minds and meditating on things true, noble, reputable, authentic, compelling, gracious--the best, not the worst; the beautiful, not the ugly; things to praise, not things to curse. Put into practice what you learned from me, what you heard and saw and realized. Do that, and God, who makes everything work together, will work you into his most excellent harmonies.

We have had some really hot days, the kind of days when it is fun to have the sprinkler on, with children running through the sprinkler, squealing because of the cold water splattering on them.

On one such day recently, a couple of children were using the hose with a nozzle on it to spray each other—laughing and squealing with delight when they were sprayed. On the nozzle, there are different positions to make the water spray at different angles, different water patterns, and different strengths of water pressure. The little five-year-old girl had the hose at one point. The spray of water wasn't quite reaching her sister. She was looking at all the various positions on the nozzle, and turned it to "Jet". She said, "That says 'Jet' – I can read now, you know!" Yes, sure enough, it did say "Jet", and sure enough, it reached her sister when she held the handle to let the water flow! She knew what it said; she knew it would spray further; and she did what she knew to do.

I thought how that so relates to our spiritual life. We can read, you know; we can understand what it says; we can do what we know to do. What we read is the important part, though. We can fill our minds with true, noble, reputable, authentic, compelling, gracious things—the best things, the beautiful things, things to praise. Or we can choose to fill our minds with the worst things, the ugly things, the things that curse. Let's fill our minds with God's Word; let's fill our minds with praise. Let's learn from others who have gone before us, those people who have set a good example, and from Jesus Himself. Life will be more harmonious if we do these things.

> _Prayer Lord Jesus, it is so easy to think about the negative things, and that can be so defeating, so discouraging, so depressing. Lord, help us to think about the positive things in our lives; help us to fill our minds with praise; help us to see the beautiful things. Amen_

My Thoughts

Joy in the Morning

Psalms 51:12 Restore to me again the joy of your salvation. (NLT)

For years, we have had robins in our neighborhood. We love to hear them sing first thing in the morning. In northern Alberta, that starts about 4:00 a.m. when dawn is breaking. They are so happy a new day has begun. I see them as praising the Lord with their song.

Last spring, blue jays moved into our neighborhood, and chased the robins away. How we missed their cheerful singing! Instead we heard the blue jays squawking during the day. I often wondered where the robins had gone. Did they have to adjust to new circumstances--maybe a new tree, or new predators like cats or barking dogs?

This year, though, the robins have returned, and are singing to their hearts' content. They are perched on the highest tree, letting the world know they are alive and well. It seems their song is a little louder, a little clearer, a little stronger than previous years.

In our lives, there are times we are singing and praising God, and everyone knows it. We are on the treetop, rejoicing in God's love and presence and acceptance. Then there are the seasons of adjusting to new circumstances, and our songs are silenced for a while. Eventually, though, our songs will return, and we will be praising God again. Likely our song will be a little louder, a little clearer, a little more confident, because it is God who gives us the song.

Nehemiah 8:10 Don't be dejected and sad, for the joy of the Lord is your strength. (NLT)

> *Prayer Dear Lord Jesus, help us to praise You. During the adjusting times in our lives, help us to trust You, knowing that Your joy will return to us. Thank You for Your joy. Amen*

My Thoughts

Lame

<u>2 Timothy 3:16</u> Every Scripture passage is inspired by God. All of them are useful for teaching, pointing out errors, correcting people, and training them for a life that has God's approval. (GW)

Last summer, we were camping with a group of family and friends. One morning, one fellow came out of his camper, only to be met face-to-face with a bear—yes, a real, live black bear—which was sitting and looking him in the eye! As soon as the bear realized that a person had appeared, he walked off into the nearby forest. As the camper watched him go, he noticed that the bear's one back leg was lame; hence, he went limping into the forest very slowly.

Later in the day, another group of campers said they had noticed a lame bear also. Again that same day, some of the children saw the lame bear too.

This poor bear, which was hurting and likely not able to catch his own food, came to a group of campers, where there was food scraps to be found--some in the garbage, maybe some just lying around, maybe some in iceboxes. He knew where to go to get food that was easily accessible. The food would also help in healing more quickly.

We are lame as well, in one way or another. Some of us may have a visible limp—a physical limp. Some of us may have emotional baggage that is weighing us down. Some may have an elderly parent who is sick. Some of us may have just lost a parent, or maybe a child, or someone close to us. Whatever it is, we are limping slowly through life.

It would be good to learn from the bear. He took the risk and came close to people, a group of humans beings, where he could find some food. We could use this same principle, and choose to come close to others, where we know we will be fed. There we will find healing; there we are more able to let go of our baggage; there we can find grace and experience God's love through others. They can help us to eat the right food, God's Word.

<u>1 Peter 2:2</u> Now, like infants at the breast, drink deep of God's pure kindness. Then you'll grow up mature and whole in God. (MSG)

> *Prayer Lord Jesus, so often, when we are hurting or weighed down, we don't want to be around people. We want to isolate ourselves, but You have built us for relationships. We need others to help us along the hard spots in life, to encourage us to eat the right kind of food. Help us to reach out to others among whom we can begin to heal. Help us most of all, to eat from Your Word the food that we so desperately need at the time. Amen*

My Thoughts

Lasting

Lamentations 3:22-23 God's loyal love couldn't have run out, his merciful love couldn't have dried up. They're created new every morning. How great your faithfulness! (MSG)

Years ago, my husband bought me a brand new full-length leather coat. I felt very special while wearing this coat. It was stylish. This coat had a zip out liner so I could wear it year round. It was very warm with the liner for winter, and also great for the cooler spring, summer and fall days, without the liner. I never changed from a winter coat to a summer coat. I just wore the same coat year in and year out. After many years, I was getting tired of wearing the same coat. It just would not wear out.

God's Word doesn't get old. God's love doesn't wear out. He doesn't get tired of loving us. He *is* love. His merciful love is created new every morning. He is faithful. Let's remember these truths as we go about our days.

Prayer Lord Jesus, thank You that Your loyal love doesn't run out. Your merciful love doesn't dry up. You are faithful. We can trust You. Help us, we pray. Amen

---

My Thoughts

Laughter

Proverbs 17:22 A cheerful disposition is good for your health; gloom and doom leave you bone-tired. (MSG)

As my parents and their siblings are passing away one at a time, I have been reminiscing about them and the fun times we had together as a family. We lived closest to my Mom's side of the family, so knew them better. One of my Mom's sisters, though, lived at the other end of the province. I remember a few times when Mom and she were together—either at our place or at her place. Oh, how I remember the fun they had! They laughed and laughed so hard. After a while, nothing was funny any more, but by then, they couldn't stop laughing. The peals of laughter filled the house!

God wants us to be happy and joyful. A cheerful disposition does good--like medicine. It is so true: when I laugh, I do feel better. Life isn't as serious; the circumstances not so pressing. God knows a good dose of laughter is for our good. So often, though, we get stuck in the gloomy side of life, and we feel bone-tired. Let's look for something to laugh about—whether it is really funny or not. We will feel better.

Prayer Lord Jesus, thank You for giving us a sense of humor and the ability to see the funny side of life. You are great! Amen

My Thoughts

Leaning Hard

<u>Song of Solomon 8:5</u> Who is this that cometh up from the wilderness, leaning upon her beloved? (KJVR)

A while back, I was struggling in many areas of my life. Everywhere I turned, I was faced with another hurdle over which to climb.

Then, one day, I read the Scripture verse for today. The bride was leaning upon her beloved. I imagine she was leaning, because she wanted to be close to him, or she was leaning for support. Maybe she was ill at the time, and needed physical support. Or perhaps she needed emotional support, or spiritual support. That day, the Lord said to me, "Lean hard. I know your burden. Lean hard, and let Me feel the pressure of your cares."

When I was at work that day, I leaned hard against the wall, picturing that wall to be Jesus Christ. I told God that I couldn't carry on, that I needed Him, and I was leaning hard on Him. He knew my burden. That was a comfort as well. Bit by bit that day, the burden lifted. Were the struggles all over? Absolutely not—but the burden was lighter.

Let's remember to lean hard on Jesus—in the bad times, but also in the good times as well.

<u>Matthew 11:28</u> "Are you tired? Worn out? Burned out on religion? Come to me. Get away with me and you'll recover your life. I'll show you how to take a real rest. (MSG)

Prayer Lord Jesus, life is rough at times, but You never promised us a rose garden. Help us to lean hard on You and trust You at all times. Amen

---

My Thoughts

Lights in the Dark

Psalms 139:23-24 Investigate my life, O God, find out everything about me; Cross-examine and test me, get a clear picture of what I'm about. See for yourself whether I've done anything wrong--then guide me on the road to eternal life. (MSG)

Over the years, we have had thirteen different international students living with us. They always bring small traditional gifts for us when they come— and often when they leave, as well.

One gift recently was a small replica of Chinese lanterns that the people carry New Year's Eve in the dark. In Taiwan, they have real candles in them. In our miniature ones, the light is battery operated. I could just imagine children being thrilled with these little lanterns. They could run into a closet and shut the door, so their lantern would light up the space inside. Then, they could run to another room, close the blinds and the door, and look into the corners of the room. What would they see, though? Would all the corners be clean, or would there be some cob webs, some dirt, something that didn't belong there, taking up space?

Jesus wants to look into the rooms in our hearts. He wants to expose every nook and cranny to His light. I wonder what He will see there. Are there cob webs that try to make fuzzy the things that God's word says are clearly wrong? Is there dirt that should be cleaned out, those cherished sins that we don't want to give up? Is there stuff stored there, like old grudges that should be thrown away? Oh, how He wants to remove those things, and to cleanse our lives from all our sin. A thought provoking question, though, is "Will we let Him shine His light into every room in our hearts?"

Prayer Lord Jesus, thank You for Your light. Like the psalmist said, investigate our lives, O God. Find out everything about us. Cross-examine and test us, and get a clear picture of what we're about. Amen

My Thoughts

Losses

Romans 8:28 That's why we can be so sure that every detail in our lives of love for God is worked into something good. (MSG)

About five years ago, I was struggling with my job with patients with Alzheimer disease, and the shift work was getting harder the older I got. So I chose to quit my job. It was a loss. Close to the same time, I had a really bad kitty that I chose to give away. This was another loss. Then shortly afterwards, my Dad passed away! Another loss! A huge loss!

The losses kept piling up. I felt overwhelmed. I had so much grieving to do. As is normal in the grieving process, I went through many emotions: anger, sadness, depression, a ray of hope, despair. It took a long time to grieve and heal.

2 Corinthians 1:3-4a All praise to the God and Father of our Master, Jesus the Messiah! Father of all mercy! God of all healing counsel! He comes alongside us when we go through hard times, and before you know it, he brings us alongside someone else who is going through hard times so that we can be there for that person just as God was there for us. (MSG)

I know now that all those losses came at the same time, so that I would lean on Jesus. He is our Comforter and Healer. He drew me to Himself during this time. All things do work together for good to those who love the Lord.

Prayer   Lord, so many times we can't see any light at the end of the tunnel. The process seems too long. Help us to claim the promises in Your Word that will comfort us. Amen

---

My Thoughts

Lying Dormant

Psalms 62:5 My soul, wait thou only upon God; for my expectation is from Him. (KJV)

Before long it will be time to think about planting fall bulbs, like tulips or crocuses or narcissus. Every time I plant some, I think about them being in the cold, frozen ground all winter. And yet in order for them to bloom beautifully in the spring, they must lie dormant all winter and wait for spring. When the warmth of the spring sun heats the ground, the bulbs grow quickly and produce bright flowers for us to enjoy.

There are times in our lives when we must lie still and wait as well. It could be a time of refocusing in our lives. Spring will come, and we will grow quickly after feeling the warmth of the Son in our hearts.

Psalms 46:10 Be still and know that I am God. (KJV)

Prayer Thank You, Jesus, for the dormant times in our lives. At times, it seems a waste of time. Help us to be still and know that You are God. Spring will come and we will bloom. Please use us to bless others. Amen

---

My Thoughts

Minor Tunes

Luke 2:11 For today in the city of David there has been born for you a Saviour, who is Christ the Lord. (NASB)

Ah! Christmas time! Part of Christmas is the music. I often sit listening, enthralled by those wonderful carols that we all have heard from childhood. Often, we know all the words for the first verse, and sometimes, the second, and third as well! Stop and listen! Can you hear the beautiful melodies of "Silent Night, Holy Night", "Hark the Herald Angels Sing", "O Come All Ye Faithful"? The harmony is beautiful! Listen! There are beautiful major chords. Did you hear the minor chords as well? Listen carefully. Ah! That is beautiful also.

That has made me think about the beauty of the Season—how Jesus willingly came to earth as a beautiful precious baby. Listen to that! It makes our hearts quicken. That is the major chords.

What about the minor chords then? They are beautiful too—in a different way. The reason for the Season is so that Jesus would grow up and die for us! Ooh! That grates on us. Listen to that chord as it is drawn out and held. The beauty in Jesus' death, burial, and resurrection could be likened to a minor chord. It was a hard thing for Him to go through—but in the end, it has brought beauty to the hearts of those who accept Him.

Ah! The Reason for the Season! When we hear those minor chords, let's praise God for sending His Son to earth for us.

> *Prayer Thank You, Lord, for the gift of music that You have given us. How we love those wonderful carols echoing through our minds at this time of year. May we be drawn closer to You at this Christmas time, thanking You for what You have done for us. Amen*

My Thoughts

Motorcycles

Psalms 31:1 In thee, O LORD, do I put my trust; let me never be ashamed: (KJV)

I have been on only a couple of motorcycles in my life. The first time is when my older brother owned a motorcycle, and he took me on a ride for a few miles in the country. I wasn't scared at all. I trusted my brother completely. It was fun. Then, as a teen-ager, I went for another ride for a few blocks in a big city. That was also fun and exhilarating. That wasn't scary either. I trusted the driver then, as well.

Now I have a chance to go on a motorcycle ride again. I have been thinking about it and feeling a bit apprehensive. I can imagine our conversation before I get on the bike. I will talk about turning corners safely, not going too fast, how to let him know if I am scared and want him to slow down. I'm not as trusting as I used to be. Oh, to be a child again! Children are so trusting.

In life, we have corners to turn, too. Maybe they are sharper than we'd like; maybe they are steeper than we'd like; maybe we are traveling faster than we'd like. How do we deal with those kinds of fears?

Psalms 37:5 Open up before GOD, keep nothing back; he'll do whatever needs to be done: (MSG)

Let's talk to God about our fears, open up to Him completely, and keep nothing back. He knows our thoughts; He knows our hearts; He knows our minds. Let's choose to trust the Lord. He is our strength and hope.

Jeremiah 17:10 But I, GOD, search the heart and examine the mind. I get to the heart of the human. I get to the root of things. I treat them as they really are, not as they pretend to be." (MSG)

> *Prayer Lord Jesus, fear can be debilitating, paralyzing. You haven't given us the spirit of fear, God. Help us to trust You in life's circumstances. Help us to take that first baby step towards You in trust. Help us to claim Your truths as our own, Lord Jesus. Help us to be completely candid with You, because You know our hearts and thoughts anyway. Speaking the truth sets us free. We love You, Jesus. Amen*

My Thoughts

Mountain Biking

Nehemiah 8:10 For the joy of the LORD is your strength. (NASB)

This summer, on one weekend, we went camping in the mountains. The further we went into the wilderness, the more I wondered if we had made a good choice to camp there. The road was rough; the way was desolate; the bridges were narrow; the tunnels were dark. What had we gotten ourselves into? Finally, late in the evening, we arrived at the camp site. Thankfully, others had gone ahead, and camp was all set up—ready for us.

There were waterfalls close by, so we all decided to bike there the next morning. It was three and one- half kilometers one way—in the mountains! Was that ever hard work going up the hills--but what fun going down the other side! We were riding on a gravel road, which made the biking harder than a paved bike trail in town. When we got to the Falls, we were exhausted! But oh, the beauty of it! It was breath-taking! We could climb up the mountain a ways, and view the Falls from a different angle. I stood in awe, filled with joy out in the wilderness with this majestic scene God had made for us. The ride back didn't seem quite so hard. Viewing the wonderful waterfalls had given us strength.

In life we have hard work to do, too. We have past hurts to deal with, and that is difficult. We have addictions to break, and that is hard work. We have wrong thought patterns that need to be changed, and that is hard. But the beauty at the end of all the hard work is breath-taking! We become a little more like Jesus after each hard task is accomplished. The hard work is worth it all.

> *Prayer Lord Jesus, sometimes life is difficult. We have things to work through and Lord, it is hard work. Help us not to faint during these times. Give us your joy, we pray. As we see in today's verse, that in turn gives us Your strength. Thank You. Amen*

My Thoughts

Mountain Climbing

Come unto me, all ye that labour and are heavy leaden, and I will give your rest. Take my yoke upon you, and learn of me; for I am meek and lowly in heart; and ye shall find rest unto your souls. For my yoke is easy, and my burden is light. (KJV)

Years ago as a teen-ager, I was at a Bible Camp in the beautiful Rocky Mountains. The highlight for me was climbing a mountain—all the way to the top. It was a semi-cloudy day when we loaded into a van to drive a few miles to the base of the mountain. Soon, we were on the upward climb. It was very hard work. Finally, after several hours, we reached the top. Oh! The beauty of it! The splendor! It was absolutely breath taking. We could see the tops of shorter mountains. We could look see taller mountains. We could look down the mountain to see where we had come from, and were amazed at the steepness, the roughness, and the hard paths on which we had come.

We were content just where we were—at the top of the mountain chosen by the camp director for us to climb. We took in the beauty of all the scenery. We soaked in the sunshine bearing down on us. At the same time, we were amazed that we had really made it. We had conquered that one mountain.

All of us have mountains to climb. They are all a different height, but we _must_ climb them. There is no shortcut in getting to the top. We can see how steep it was; we can see how rugged it was; we can see how rough it was.

There are so many different mountains to climb—fear, sickness, abuse, rejection, death of a loved one, denial, betrayal. We can choose to stay at the bottom of the mountain, or we can choose to climb the mountains. After all the hard work of climbing through abuse, or rejection, or betrayal, we can relax, and enjoy the _Son_ shining upon us at the top of the mountain. We can bask in the warmth of His love. Then we will know it was worth it all.

> _Prayer Oh, Lord Jesus, it is so hard climbing a mountain. it seems, we no sooner reach the summit of one that we have to start all over on another one. We must keep going in order to bask in Your Sonlight. Thank You that You are always with us. Thank You, Lord Jesus._

My Thoughts

Mowing

Psalms 72:6 He shall come down like rain upon the mown grass: as showers that water the earth. (KJV)

Ah! Spring has sprung! How I love to watch everything come to live once again. As the grass is growing, we know sooner or later, that it will have to be mowed. In fact, first thing in the spring when the ground has dried up, we mow our lawn very, very short. It greens up so quickly after that. Then, it has to be mowed every week—sometimes twice a week, depending on how much rain and heat we have. Even though the grass is cut, it doesn't give up and quit growing. It just keeps doing what God wants it to do—and that is to grow. It is beautiful. There is no way to have a velvety, even lawn without repeated mowings over the summer. And oh, how the grass needs rain in order to grow.

In our lives, we get mowed often too—some pain here, some disappointment there, or the loss of someone dear to us. Yes, it is hard. Then God sends showers of warm rain upon us as we are struggling with being mown. This is a time for us to develop sympathy, tenderness, evenness in our lives. Our lives keep growing, doing what God wants us to do.

When we get mown to one degree or another, let's not dread those times. They are sure to be followed by the rain and growth.

> Prayer Lord Jesus, we dread the mowing times in our lives. They aren't easy. They aren't fun. It is really tough. Help us to look to You, knowing that You will send the warm rain into our souls to make us grow. Amen

My Thoughts

Neighborhood Barbecue

Luke 6:38 Give away your life; you'll find life given back, but not merely given back--given back with bonus and blessing. Giving, not getting, is the way. Generosity begets generosity." (MSG)

We have had a neighborhood barbecue. It was arranged through our church. The food and drinks were supplied. All I had to do was go to pick them up. This was a church-wide event so the announcement was made in church. The plan was for people who lived in each neighborhood to be made aware of the location of various barbecues throughout the city, and go to enjoy the food and fellowship closest to them.

It had been a busy day, a busy week, a busy month. I was tired. The weather wasn't that great. It was cool and cloudy. I was complaining bitterly on the inside. Something I don't like is to be outside when it is cold. Oh, how I begrudged the time that I had to spend setting up for the barbecue, lighting the barbecue, making sure all preparations were complete. I was not a happy camper, although I put on a happy face.

Then, neighbors started coming. Some, whom I had never met before, arrived around the corner of the house. Others, whom we had known for a few years, came, excited to reconnect with us as well. Bit by bit, my attitude changed. I was really having fun. Guess what? It rained on us also. By then, it didn't matter to me. My heart was warmed by friends—old and new.

I thought about my previous rotten attitude. I did give of my time, my home, and myself. And how I was blessed! It thrilled my heart anew to know that God's Word is so true, as in our verse for today.

Oh, how God longs to bless us but sometimes, we block that blessing by not giving of ourselves.

Prayer Lord Jesus, so many times, we don't see the whole picture. We see only the immediate circumstances. Often all we see is ourselves. Please forgive us, we pray. We know Your Word is true. So God, we are depending on You to give our life back with bonus and blessing when we give of ourselves. We love You, Jesus. Amen

---

My Thoughts

New Ruts

<u>Proverbs 4:26</u> Carefully consider the path for your feet, and all your ways will be established. (HCSB)

We had an unbelievably long winter this year with record amounts of snow. From the first snow fall till the snow was mostly melted was six long months. We also had seven feet of snow last year – the most we have had in over seventy years. Because of that, our streets were a mess.

Snow was packed down on the streets very deeply. Every time it snowed, it would get packed down a bit more, a bit deeper until there was twelve to eighteen inches of hard-packed snow on which we were driving. When it got a bit warmer, the weight of the vehicles would then make a rut. In the residential areas of town, we would all drive in the same spot, making the rut deeper and deeper as the days progressed. When we were in the rut, it would throw our vehicle back and forth as we followed the rut. There wasn't much we could do about it.

Then, I noticed that some of the drivers were driving a few inches beside the deep rut. That way, they weren't in the rut – they were above the rut. It took a lot of effort not to go into the rut, in the first place, and then, to stay out of the rut took a lot of concentration. What happened, though, was interesting. It wasn't long until there was a new rut being formed. It was also getting deeper as time went on. Once we were driving in the new rut, it also threw our vehicle around; but, it was a new rut. Maybe it was a better rut.

I thought so many times, we get into a rut in our lives. It is a habit; it is easy; it is comfortable; it is what we know. It could be the way we speak to others; it could be our attitude towards situations in life; it could be the way we spend our free time. Whatever it is, it is all we know, and we feel safe there. It is very hard to get out of the well-known rut and change some things in our lives. The old rut is so engraved in our way of life. Oh, let's be mindful of the old, destructive ruts in our lives, and learn new, healthy ways to live.

> *Prayer Oh, Lord, so many times we don't realize we are in an unhealthy rut, until we see some damage caused by what we have done or not done. Help us, we pray, to keep our eyes on You and to learn new ways of living, in order to bring honor and glory to Your name. We want to be like You, Jesus. We humble ourselves before You. Amen*

My Thoughts

Our Needs

<u>Philippians 4:19</u> You can be sure that God will take care of everything you need, his generosity exceeding even yours in the glory that pours from Jesus. (MSG)

Years ago, when our children were younger, we were very hard up. My husband was pastoring a church, as well as working night shift, in order to keep us fed and clothed. We wore second-hand clothes; I made bread, cakes, cookies; we grew a huge garden, and froze and canned all the produce from it. We ate ground meat, sausages, and hot dogs for meat. We drank powdered milk. We were definitely on a budget. Even though we spent our money wisely, often we would have no flour to make the bread, or nothing in the cupboards for supper except rolled oats to make porridge.

God was so faithful, though. I can't count the number of times I would go to the door, and find a bag of flour, or a bag of groceries sitting on our step. One time, a friend gave me a couple of brand new dresses that she thought would suit me, and they did! They fit perfectly too! We would go to garage sales, and find just what we needed for clothing. God definitely supplied all of our needs. It was a neat learning time for us.

Let's ever keep in mind that God does supply our needs—our food, our clothing, our homes, our cars, our jobs. He supplies our spiritual and emotional needs as well. Great is the Lord!

Prayer Thank You, Lord Jesus, that you do take care of everything we need. You are so generous. Amen

---

My Thoughts

Pain!

Pain! Emotional pain! Physical pain! Financial pain! Spiritual pain! We all go through some kind of pain in our lives!

Quite a few years ago, I was in a lot of pain in many areas of my life. I was in pain from morning till night. I was in pain all night long. All I knew was pain. Because the process was so long, I questioned God, and wondered why I had to go through all that, and others didn't. What I didn't see at the time is that everyone has pain—just in different areas and different levels at one time or another in their lives.

The pain got so bad that I knew I needed help, so went for Christian counseling. During this time of dealing with my personal issues, the pain increased in some areas before it got better. I had to accept the pain, and the process of dealing with the pain as a learning tool for me. It was then that I found a couple of verses that I love.

2 Corinthians 1:3-4 Blessed be God, even the Father of our Lord Jesus Christ, the Father of mercies, and the God of all comfort; Who comforteth us in all our tribulation, that we may be able to comfort them which are in any trouble, by the comfort wherewith we ourselves are comforted of God. (KJV)

The truths of those verses were life-changing for me. I claimed them as mine. God was comforting me so that I could reach out and comfort others. There was a purpose for my pain.

I would like to suggest that any pain we have is for a purpose. Physical pain causes us to go to the doctor. Spiritual pain causes us to run to God. Financial pain causes us to seek help in that area. Emotional pain causes us to find someone to help us through those rough times.

God is our comfort in every area of our lives. No matter what the pain, He is there for us—every minute of every day.

Prayer   Oh God, how we resist pain in our lives! Often, we rebel against it. But God, You are omnipresent. Help us to claim Your Word, knowing that You will comfort us, and then You want us to go and comfort others with the same comfort with which You have comforted us. You are so great, Lord! Help us to run to You quickly in our pain. Thank You. Amen

My Thoughts

Pansies

<u>John 7:37</u> On the last and greatest day of the Feast, Jesus stood and said in a loud voice, "If anyone is thirsty, let him come to me and drink. (NIV)

I was sitting out in my yard enjoying the beautiful warm day. I was soaking in the sunshine, as were the flowers in my backyard. As I was looking at each of them, I noticed that some of my gorgeous orange pansies were wilting in the heat. I was quite amazed, because we had had several heavy showers that week. Then I realized that the rain had come from the other direction, so the flowers along the east side of the house hadn't had the opportunity to be refreshed by the plenteous showers the other plants had enjoyed on the west side of the house.

I quickly got the hose out and watered them sufficiently. In a short while, they looked so much better. As I was watering them, I thought about how desperately we need the refreshing water of the Word of God so that we won't wilt under the hot trials in life. My pansies had rain around them, but it didn't help. God's Words around us won't suffice either. Oh, let's go to the fountain often and drink! We will be refreshed.

<u>Matthew 5:6</u> Blessed are those who hunger and thirst for righteousness, for they will be filled. (NIV)

Prayer Thank You, God, for this lesson in nature. We don't want to wilt. We want to grow. Help us to be ever mindful of drinking from Your fountain to quench our thirst. Amen

---

My Thoughts

Photography

Isaiah 52:12 But you don't have to be in a hurry. You're not running from anybody! GOD is leading you out of here. (MSG)

Psalms 46:10 Be still, and know that I am God. (KJVR)

Isn't it fun trying to take a picture of little children? One child, at a time, is often a challenge. It is hard for them to sit still long enough to take a good picture. I have seen many small children gathered together--with the adults trying to take a picture. One baby would crawl away, another one would cry, another one would make a face. The parents were telling the little ones, "Just sit still for a jiffy! It won't take long!" Oh, the challenge of it all. Yes, the final picture looked quite natural with all these little people. The finished product, though, wasn't necessarily what the adults had in mind. They would have preferred the little ones to sit still, so that all of their faces were in the picture rather than someone crawling away, quite oblivious to the task at hand. The picture that was taken was a distinct likeness to the children.

Sometimes, God tells us not to hurry. He tells us to sit still. We usually have a hard time doing that. Often, we want to do something to be Christians, when all we need to do is let Him work in us, because we are already Christians.

God's eternal purpose for us is that we will be like His Son—just as a picture is like the ones who are posing. In order for this to happen, there are times we need to not be in a hurry, to be still and know that God is God.

Prayer Lord Jesus, so many times we get in a rush and we don't have time for You. Please forgive us. Help us to listen to Your still small voice, and be still when You tell us to. Amen

---

My Thoughts

Piano versus Synth

<u>James 4:10</u> Humble yourselves in the presence of the Lord, and He will exalt you. (NASB)

<u>2 Timothy 3:16</u> Every part of Scripture is God-breathed and useful one way or another--showing us truth, exposing our rebellion, correcting our mistakes, training us to live God's way.(MSG)

I have struggled with learning to play the synthesizer in our church band. It has been a huge stretching time for me.

As time went on, I felt more comfortable playing it. Then the opportunity came to play the piano in the band rather than the synth. It was scary, but I was more used to a piano so felt okay with it. During practice, the regular pianist came and corrected me with my timing. She said to listen for the snare drum. I was completely overwhelmed. I didn't know what the snare sounded like! There were so many instruments to listen to, so many sounds to hear, so much going on! I had to do as I was instructed, even though it was difficult. I did make it through the morning service. But it was another huge stretching time for me. I had to humble myself and take instruction from someone who knows much more about music than I do.

God knows much more about our lives than we do. He gave us an instruction manual as well. He knows how to instruct us. He longs to instruct us. Let's humble ourselves and listen to what He has to say.

Prayer Lord Jesus, thank You for Your instruction manual, the Word of God. Help us to read it. Help us to humble ourselves and listen to Your instructions for us. Then help us to do as You instruct us. We need You and Your power today. Amen

---

My Thoughts

Placebos

Philippians 4:19 But my God shall supply all your need according to his riches in glory by Christ Jesus. (KJV)

There have been times in my life that I just can't go to sleep quickly. When I do finally drift off, it is a restless sleep. I toss and turn all night. In the morning, I don't feel rested at all. If this happens too many nights in a row, I become anxious about not being able to sleep, and I lie awake even longer. One night recently, I tossed and turned for a couple of hours. About midnight, I got up and took a couple of Tylenol. When I crawled back into bed, I fell right to sleep, had a wonderful sleep, and felt good in the morning.

God spoke to me about that during the day. I heard loudly and clearly that I was depending on the Tylenol, and not depending on God for my need of sleep. That night as I crawled into bed, I choose not to take any Tylenol. Instead, I held a pretend pill in my hand, put it in my mouth and swallowed it. I said aloud that this pill is God's peace. The next placebo I swallowed was God's rest. The placebos continued for a while. They were God's love for me, God's acceptance of me, God's compassion for me. I laid my head down on my pillow, closed my eyes, and drifted right off to sleep, and slept like a baby. I was so amazed.

What do we depend on to meet out needs? Is it our careers, our families, our homes? What are the pills we take to give us the rest we so desperately long for and need? So many times, we lose sight of the Pill-Giver. How we long to feel His presence, His peace, His comfort. Jesus is patiently waiting for us to turn to Him, and He will gladly fill all our needs.

Prayer Lord Jesus, thank You that You will supply all our needs—not just some, or a few, or most--but all. Help us to cling to that promise You have given us. Amen

---

My Thoughts

Priorities

<u>*Deuteronomy 17:19*</u> That scroll is to remain at his side at all times; he is to study it every day so that he may learn what it means to fear his GOD, living in reverent obedience before these rules and regulations by following them. (MSG)

First thing in the morning when I arise, I want to dash to the computer, and read my email. I want to see who has written. It could be a sibling, it could be a friend, it could be an acquaintance. Then I want to see what they have written. Do they have good news? Bad news? What is in the email? Will it be news of family? Friends? Will they share a heart ache? A triumph? What will it be? I am interested in hearing from others and sharing in their joys or their trials. It is a priority in my life.

God sends me mail every day, too. I have it in my desk drawer, waiting to be read. It is new and fresh every day. I can read one portion today and learn something. The next day, I can read the same portion, and learn something new from it. I have a few different versions. There are times I run out the door before I read God's message to me. God wants to speak to me every day, through His Holy Word.

May we not neglect reading the message that God has sent to us. It is written in love. It shares joys, struggles, victories, heart aches, discouragements. We can relate to these messages to us. We read His message by delving into the Bible, reading devotionals, or doing a Bible study. He is anxious to speak to us. Are we as anxious to hear from Him?

<u>*1 Chronicles 16:11*</u> Seek the LORD and His strength; Seek His face continually. (NASB)

> *Prayer Lord Jesus, Your Word is written to us to help us along our journey. You tell us You love us, and that is so important to know. You give us instruction about how to live. You tell us of struggles and victories of those gone before us, so that we can learn from them. Thank You, Jesus. Amen*

My Thoughts

Rear-View Mirror

Hebrews 12:2 Keep your eyes on Jesus, who both began and finished this race we're in. Study how he did it. Because he never lost sight of where he was headed--that exhilarating finish in and with God--he could put up with anything along the way: cross, shame, whatever. And now he's there, in the place of honour, right alongside God. (MSG)

As I drive, I often check the rear-view mirror. The purpose, of course, is to drive more safely. I need to see if another vehicle is coming up behind me, or if someone is in the lane beside me before I change lanes. Of course, what I see in the mirror is where I have been.

In comparison to the windshield, the rear-view mirror is very tiny. I can't drive forward while constantly looking in the rear-view mirror. It is only for quick looks in order to drive safely.

Looking at our past can be likened to looking in the rear-view mirror. We can see where we've been. We can't keep going forward, though, if we constantly look at our past. That will cause problems—just like looking into the rear-view mirror in our cars in order to drive forwards—it just doesn't work. Off and on through life, we get a glimpse of our past. We make choices at that point—whether to become better or bitter. We can choose to forgive. We can choose to drive straight ahead and follow Christ.

Ephesians 4:32 Be gentle with one another, sensitive. Forgive one another as quickly and thoroughly as God in Christ forgave you. (MSG)

Joshua 24:15 "If it is disagreeable in your sight to serve the LORD, choose for yourselves today whom you will serve: whether the gods which your fathers served which were beyond the River, or the gods of the Amorites in whose land you are living; but as for me and my house, we will serve the LORD." (NASB)

> *Prayer Lord Jesus, we all have a past. We all have good and bad parts of our past. Help us not to get stuck there, though. Help us to make the right choices and keep following You. Amen*

My Thoughts

Reasoning with God

Job 23:6-7 Would He contend with me by the greatness of His power? No, surely He would pay attention to me. There the upright would reason with Him; and I would be delivered forever from my Judge. (NASB)

I'm sure we have all had times with family or friends that we need to reason things out with them. I remember a few years ago, when I was trying to reason some difficult things out with some friends. None of us was seeing the others' view point at all. It caused a lot of hard feelings. It seemed that they weren't paying attention to what I was saying, and maybe they felt the same way about me. Were we not willing to try to understand the others' viewpoints? I don't know.

What I do know is that God is always going to pay attention to us. In today's Scripture, Job reflects on the great truth that the upright are able to reason with God. That tells me that I need to be honest with God. I can reason with Him and He will listen to me. It amazes me that a righteous God is willing to listen to me and hear my side of the story. He doesn't judge me nor condemn me. He allows me to say what I need to tell Him. And yes, He reasons with me. He talks very plainly to me. How I praise Him for that!

Let's remember that God will always pay attention to us—no matter what spot we are at in our lives. He will listen to us, and we can reason with Him.

Prayer Thank you, Lord, for paying attention to us. Thank You for listening to us. Thank You for allowing us to reason with You. You are a great God. We love You. Amen

My Thoughts

Recovery

Galatians 6:2 Bear one another's burdens and so fulfill the law of Christ. (KJV)

I have joined a gym recently. There are a few extra pounds that I need to get rid of. The gym has thirteen different machines on which to exercise. They are all in a circle. In between each of those machines is a recovery board. The goal is to work as hard as I can on the machines, and then, "recover" on the boards by running on the spot.

I am also involved in Celebrating Recovery at our church. We all need recovery-- some of us from co-dependency; some from drug abuse; some from generational things in our families. During recovery, there is a lot of hard work to do. We have to face denial, and learn how to break that in our lives. We know we are powerless to change anything in our lives. It is only through Jesus Christ, Who gives us strength and power, that we can do these things. It is God who changes our hearts.

As I looked at this recovery process, and the "recovery" boards at the gym, I saw a likeness to the two. At the gym, we work hard; we struggle with doing as many repetitions on a machine as possible; we feel weak and faint at times on those machines. But then we go the recovery boards where we can relax somewhat and catch our breath. We need those "recovery" times to keep going.

So, too, in celebrating recovery. We work hard at breaking denial; we work hard at doing our inventory; we choose to forgive others, and that is hard work. And yet, there is the "recovery" boards as well. We each have our accountability partner on whom to lean. We have a sponsor to support us. We can be honest and real with them, and they still love us and accept us. I am sure we could never make it through this process without these "recovery" boards on whom to rely. Praise God for others who are there for us to help us in the recovery process.

> *Prayer Lord Jesus, thank You that You show us the things in our lives from which we need to recover. Help us to do the hard work of recovery. Thank You that You have put people in our lives for us to rely on as we go through this process. Amen*

My Thoughts

Rejoice

Philippians 4:4 Rejoice in the Lord always; and again, I say rejoice. (NASB)

John 10:28-30 I give them real and eternal life. They are protected from the Destroyer for good. No one can steal them from out of my hand. The Father who put them under my care is so much greater than the Destroyer and Thief. No one could ever get them away from him. (MSG)

I am told that when my older sister started school, she would sit down and teach me the alphabet, how to print, how to sound the letters. She also taught me the notes on the piano when she started taking piano lessons. She was a very good teacher. I have no recollection of this at all. I have wondered why I don't remember that. Neither do I remember some of the hard times that we went through as a family. Where has my memory gone?

The things I do remember are mostly from when I was ten. That is the year that I accepted the Lord. That is the year that I started piano lessons. That is the year that we moved into our new home that Dad built. These, as well as my sister teaching me so many things, are all good things to remember.

All this makes me very conscious that I should obey today's Scripture to rejoice in the Lord always. The command to rejoice is repeated twice in one verse. I see that as God emphasizing the importance of rejoicing. I think I need to rejoice that I don't remember the hard times.

God wants us to rejoice in Him, not in the circumstances of our lives. He is always with us to lead and guide us.

Hebrews 13:5 I will never desert you, nor will I ever forsake you. (NASB)

Prayer Lord, for some reason we don't remember all the things that happened in our lives. We know that You have given us real and eternal life. Thank You that You protect us, and no one can steal us from Your hands. Help us to keep our eyes on You, and to rejoice in You—during the good times as well as the bad—during the times we remember and the times we have forgotten. Thank You. Amen

My Thoughts

Relationship Swing

<u>*Matthew 11:28-30*</u> "Come to Me, all who are weary and heavy-laden, and I will give you rest. Take My yoke upon you and learn from Me, for I am gentle and humble in heart, and YOU WILL FIND REST FOR YOUR SOULS. For My yoke is easy and My burden is light." (NASB)

I have a wonderful piece of furniture on my patio in the backyard. It is a swing that two or three people can sit. It has a canopy to offer shade from the hot sun. I love sitting there and enjoying the smells of springtime, the sounds of the summer out-of-doors, and the sight of the clear blue sky.

Often, my family, my friends, or my neighbors are sitting there with me. As we drink a glass of iced water or lemonade, we talk. We share our lives with each other. We share our victories and our struggles. We laugh with each other and cry with each other. Sometimes we pray. There's something about sitting outside, gently swinging that causes us to be candid. I have named this special spot "My Relationship Swing". I cherish the moments I spend with others there. We are building relationships.

<u>*John 1:12*</u> But as many as received Him, to them He gave the right to become children of God, even to those who believe in His name. (NASB)

God is a God of relationships. First of all, He wants a relationship with us. Then He wants us to have relationships with others. We need others—for acceptance, for love, for sharing without judgment. How lonely life would be without Him and without other people.

Yet it takes time to build relationships. Let's be consistent in building our relationship with God and with others.

> *Prayer Lord Jesus, thank You that You are a God of relationships— first, a relationship with You, and then with others. You never intended for us to do life alone. Help us, we pray to build those healthy relationships. Amen*

My Thoughts

Rests

Matthew 14:13 When Jesus got the news, he slipped away by boat to an out-of-the-way place by himself. (MSG)

I remember well the excitement of starting piano lessons. I still have the little beginner book: "Here we go, up a row, to a birthday party"—all played on three notes in the right hand. Then there followed "Dolly dear, Sandman's near, You will soon be sleeping"—all played with the left hand, on three notes. Then as I progressed through the book, how exciting it was to play with both hands. Then I learned a piece with staccatos, and then a piece with one sharp—and then one flat. And oh, the thrill of learning one with rests in it. I had to learn to count that rest as if it were a note and then continue on with the song. It was exciting for me.

As I learned more and more and went on to the next level, there were more songs with more rests, different lengths of rest, some in the right hand, some in the left, and some together. I loved learning all of this. Those rests are what made each song what it was. The composer knew the exact spot where a rest was needed to complete the melody that he wanted to create.

In our lives, we need rests as well. Those rests come in many forms. We need our sleep every night. We often need a break during the day to rest. Rests can sometimes come in the form of sickness, disappointed plans or frustrated efforts. But rests they are. God is writing the music of our lives. He knows when we need those rests in order to compose the song He wants us to sing with our lives. Let's trust Him as He composes the song of our lives, and praise Him along the way as He is doing it.

Prayer Lord Jesus, sometimes we are so weary and we wonder how we can carry on another day, another hour, another minute. It is Your work we are doing but we are tired. At times, we think that we can't stop to rest. It is exciting to know that You are composing the song of our lives, and You are doing it exactly the way it will sound the best. Help us to stop and listen to Your music during those resting times of our lives. Thank You for composing the song. May we let You do it as You will. Amen

My Thoughts

Return to the Lord

Isaiah 51:11 Therefore the redeemed of the Lord shall return, and come with singing unto Zion. (KJV)

Most little children love to be held and hugged. As a mother and grandmother, I have noticed over the years, though, that there comes a time (usually during the teen years) that we don't want to be hugged any more. As adults, it is good to respect that choice that others make. We will be waiting lovingly for them to come back and want a hug. We want to hug them even though they don't want our hugs right now. When others are struggling, we especially want to hug them to let them know we care.

Most of us have seasons in our lives when we don't want to be hugged by others or by God. It could be due to being independent, or rebellious, or bitter, or a number of other reasons. Whatever the reason, God is waiting patiently for us to run to Him for a hug, whether we are struggling or not. How He longs to hug us to let us know He cares. He bought us and loves us more than we can fathom.

Isaiah 44:22 b Return unto me; for I have redeemed thee. (KJV)

Prayer Lord Jesus, thank You that You wait patiently for us to come to You. Oh, how we need to know You care every hour. Amen

---

My Thoughts

Robin Eggs

John 1:12 But as many as received him to them gave he power to become the sons of God, even to them that believe on his name. (KJV)

One of my clients lives on an acreage a few miles out of town. They have beautiful trees and flowers all around their yard. Beside the deck stands a tall cedar tree, in which is found a perfectly round little nest. When I first saw it, there were two beautiful blue robin eggs in it. The next time I was there, the eggs had hatched, and in the nest were two naked little baby robins. For those eggs to hatch, the shells had to be broken. The babies had to do some hard work and peck their way out of the hard shells.

The baby robins were kind of ugly, but someday, they would be beautiful adult robins, with an orange breast if they are males. They will resemble their parents. The purpose of the robins' mating is to produce some more of their kind, to be just like them.

I would like to suggest that in our lives, we have to do some hard work and break the outer shell as well. The outer shell could be very beautiful like the blue robin eggs. But it has to be broken in order for the new to be seen. At first, that inner self could be ugly, just like the baby robins. As we grow spiritually, we will become more and more beautiful and become like Jesus. That is His purpose for us.

> _Prayer Lord, the outer shell being broken can be very painful. Seeing the ugly part of us is painful as well. Help us to trust You, knowing that something beautiful will adorn us later. That something is You. Thank You. Amen_

My Thoughts

Roots

Psalms 32:11 So rejoice in the Lord and be glad, all you who obey Him! Shout for joy, all you whose hearts are pure! (NLT)

I have known people who have had warts on the bottom of their feet. They are very painful. Even after going to the doctor, there is still pain. Usually the procedure is for the doctor to scrape off the tops. That does help for a short time, but soon, they grow and are painful again. At some point, the doctor may suggest putting some "stuff" on them to help remove the root. That can be even more painful. People suffer for months with sore feet. Only when the root is gone will anyone have lasting comfort, and then walking is not painful.

I thought how much those warts are like "roots" in our lives. They can be roots of unforgiveness, resentment and bitterness. There can be roots of physical abuse, sexual abuse, and verbal abuse. There can be roots of doubt, rejection, and shame. There can be roots of discouragement, despair, and depression. There can be roots of insecurity, abandonment, no self worth.

Most times, we live with those roots continuing to grow deep into the recesses of our souls. Often, only when the pain of living with the roots is bad enough, will we do anything about it. At times, we try to fix the surface problem by ourselves. Scraping the tops of the warts doesn't help. Applying ointment to the top doesn't help. Only God can help.

We need the Great Physician to expose the roots in our lives, and allow Him to dig them out. Then, and only then, will the pain be gone, and we can walk with joy.

> _Prayer Lord Jesus, so many times we wrestle with pain caused from roots in our lives. Please expose those roots to us and break the denial in our lives. Please help us to allow You to do the healing in our lives that we need. Amen_

My Thoughts

Rustling Leaves

Psalms 96:12 Let Wilderness turn cartwheels, Animals, come dance, Put every tree of the forest in the choir. (MSG)

When the children were young, I used to love going camping. They enjoyed it so much. The freedom to run and play was exhilarating—for them as well as for us, the parents who were watching close by. Often, we would see squirrels or chipmunks dashing around also—up this tree, down that one, and over to another one. It was fun to watch them scurrying around. Sometimes, we would leave food out for them and sit quietly while watching them come to eat what we offered them. I wonder how many more little animals were watching from their protection of trees and underbrush.

It was so peaceful and quiet out in the bush; sometimes miles from any civilization at all. There were no phones ringing, no televisions on, no radios playing: complete silence--except for the rustling of the leaves in the light breeze in the evening, or the sound of little animals dashing though the forest, or the brook close by. Oh, how I enjoyed that part of camping. It was like God was speaking softly to me. I could hear Him saying, "I have made this creation, this forest, these animals, the quietness, the rippling brook nearby--all for you to enjoy."

Psalms 96:11 Let's hear it from Sky, With Earth joining in, And a huge round of applause from Sea. (MSG)

God has given us so much beauty in our lives, if only we will look and really see it. Let's slow down long enough to enjoy the beauty that is close to us—not only while we are on vacation. The sky is beautiful and changing every minute of the day. Let's praise God for the beauty of His creation.

Ecclesiastes 3:11a He has made everything beautiful in its time. (ESV)

> _Prayer Thank You, God, for the beauty that You have placed all around us. Sometimes, life seems so hard and so dark that we can't see the wonderful things all around us. Help us to focus on You and the things You have made for us to enjoy. Amen_

My Thoughts

Sanded

Philippians 1:6 God is the one who began this good work in you, and I am certain that he won't stop before it is complete on the day that Christ Jesus returns. (CEV)

My husband works with wood; he does all kinds of woodworking. He has renovated our home; he makes tables for others; he builds shelves or walls where needed at work. Furniture is the thing that he likes to build. He has built shelves, and coffee tables, and entertainment centers, and a number of other things.

The one thing in common with all wood work is that the rough wood has to be finished. There are nail holes that need to be filled. The roughness has to be smoothed. The procedure to achieve the desired effect is that the wood has to be sanded. It is a big job. I have watched my husband during this process. He sands for a while, then stops and runs his hand over the sanded area to see how it feels. It might still be a little rough, so he sands some more. He keeps repeating this until the wood has the desired smoothness. He then stains it and varnishes it to produce the finished product.

This is so much like our lives. God looks at us and sees the finished product. But we aren't finished yet. We have a few holes to be filled. We have rough spots to be sanded. I can picture Jesus looking down, rubbing those sanded areas, to see how smooth we are becoming. Maybe it isn't quite right, so we are sanded a bit more. Eventually, that area is okay but there is another one that should be sanded as well. The process continues all through life. When we reach glory, God will look at us, pleased with His finished work in us.

> _Prayer Lord Jesus, thank You that You work in our lives. You sand this area and that area. Even though the sanding times aren't pleasant, we do yield to those times and accept them as from You for our good, and for Your glory. Amen_

My Thoughts

Saskatoons

Psalms 37:4 Delight yourself in the LORD; And He will give you the desires of your heart. (NASB)

Saskatoon season is approaching soon. Saskatoons are small purple berries that grow in clusters on bushes. Because they grow in the wild, we have to go scouting around to find them. Many years, we have tramped through trees and undergrowth to get to them. At such moments, filling a bucket of saskatoons is our hearts' desire. We can almost taste the pies made with them.

Our buckets, though, are not instantly nor easily filled. We have some hard work to do. We see large clusters at the top of some of the trees. It is hard to get to the tree. Then it is hard to pull it down. Often, we are disappointed because the clusters that looked so big up there are not really as big once we have pulled the tree down. It takes a long time to fill a bucket, one cluster at a time. That isn't all the work, either. Once we get them home, there's picking out the bad ones, washing the good ones, sorting, and cleaning for a long time. This is also a lot of work.

But—the pies are wonderful, the muffins are the best, the desserts are great! While eating them, then we know it was worth it all.

Life's journey is hard too. We have to trudge through underbrush at times. Sometimes, we have to pull down strongholds. Life can be tedious while we pursue our hearts' desire.

The song, _When We See Christ_, by Esther Kerr Rusthoi, says it well:

> It will be worth it all, when we see Jesus.
> Life's trials will seem so small, when we see Christ.
> One glimpse of His dear face, all sorrow will erase.
> So bravely run the race, till we see Christ.

Prayer Oh, Lord, life can be so hard. Help us to keep Your face ever before us. Amen

My Thoughts

School Years

Philippians 1:6 For I am confident of this very thing, that He who began a good work in you will perfect it until the day of Christ Jesus. (NASB)

As another school year has started, I have been reminiscing about my school years and those of my children. How exciting it was to go back to school the first day of September!

As a child, I would always have a new outfit to wear to school the first day. I remember my mother finishing up a new dress after I went to bed. Oh, the excitement of getting up in the morning and seeing my new dress hanging there ready to put on! Mom would look on with glee as I modeled my new dress, and she would be proud of her accomplishment.

Then, of course, there were shoes to buy. Often my old ones would be a way too small and even hurting my feet a little bit before the new school year started. That was because I was growing –which is good and normal. Every year, I was a bit taller and needed new clothes.

It is also good and normal for us to grow as Christians and become more like Jesus. Yes, sometimes, it hurts—just like my old shoes. Hurts can come in many forms. They can be such things as rejection, judgment, or harsh words spoken to us. Hurts can be financial--when we don't know where our next dollar is coming from. Hurts can be physical—a pain, a sickness, a disease. God knows which hurt fits us in order to make us grow. Bit by bit, we do grow and have a new wardrobe—one that pleases Jesus more every year— and one that will be perfect some day in heaven.

Prayer Jesus, we don't like hurting, but we do want to grow. It seems that often the two go together. Help us to have the eternal view when life hurts, knowing that You are looking on, and are pleased that we are growing to become like You. Thank You. Amen

My Thoughts

Secrets

Psalm 90:8 You place our sins before you, our secret sins where you can see them. (GNB)

In our town, in our province, in our country, summer is the time to repair the side roads, the streets, the highways. During winter time, it cannot be done. So the construction is in full strength during the summer months. It is very frustrating when trying to go across town, or across the province, for that matter.

Basically, we human beings are impatient—we want to get to where we are going and to do it quickly. I see that so much more in our booming city. We all have a purpose for our travels, and it is hard to slow down for those construction zones. It is not safe for the workers when the motorists go by so fast. As a result, the law now states that the speeding fines are doubled when workers are present.

I received an interesting letter in the mail not long ago. I opened it and was surprised to see that it was a speeding ticket. It showed a picture of my car, the license plate number, the street I had been on, and the amount of the fine. I couldn't remember when I had last been on that street. But I couldn't deny it—the car's picture was in front of my eyes; the license plate number matched mine. I had to admit that I had been speeding, and I had to pay my fine—yes, my doubled fine.

I thought about how God says, "Be sure your sin will catch up with you." *(Numbers 32:23 Holman Christian Standard Bible)* When that happens, we can deny it, or we can minimize it, or we can blame others for our sin. Even if we continue to live in denial about our sins, God still sees them. They are not hidden from Him at all. Alternatively, we can acknowledge our sin and agree with God that it is sin, and He will cleanse us.

1 John 1:9 On the other hand, if we admit our sins--make a clean breast of them--he won't let us down; he'll be true to himself. He'll forgive our sins and purge us of all wrongdoing. (MSG)

Even if we continue to live in denial about our sins, God still sees them. They are not hidden from Him at all.

<u>Numbers 32:23</u> Be sure your sin will catch up with you. (HCSB)

Prayer Lord Jesus, help us to be honest with You and with others about our sins. Amen

My Thoughts

Seeing Jesus

<u>*Revelation 22:4*</u> And they will see his face. (NLT)

Recently at the airport, I saw such a beautiful picture. A young lady was pacing back and forth, waiting for the arrival of the aircraft. When it was announced that the passengers would soon be entering the terminal, she stood still and waited as close to the door as possible. Before long, a tall, handsome young man rushed in through the gate. The young lady only had eyes for him, rushed to him, and they embraced. I don't know how long he had been gone or where he had been, but the joy in seeing each other was definitely visible.

I'm sure our eyes will be on Jesus as we enter the pearly gates, and we will rush to Him and tell Him how much we love Him. What a blessed thought to see Jesus face to face--He Who loves us and died for us.

Prayer Lord Jesus, we are on a journey here. Some of us have a longer journey ahead than others. But our destination is the same. As Christians, we will walk through the gates and see You. Thank You for providing the way and for being the pilot of our aircraft. Amen

My Thoughts

Self-Worth

<u>2 Corinthians 5:17</u> Therefore if any man be in Christ, he is a new creature: old things are passed away; behold, all things are become new. (KJV)

In one computer game I play, the computer talks to me. The computer voice is actually quite irritating. The messages it gives me, though, are encouraging. It tells me, "Awesome", "Good move", "Level completed". I feel good about myself every time I hear the compliments. It boosts my confidence level. Of course, I am being encouraged to go to the next level. This is all good and fine in the computer world, but I mustn't depend on that for my sense of self-worth.

Often in life, our self-worth comes from pleasing others, or driving ourselves to reach the top of the ladder, or having the fanciest home, or biggest motor home, or fastest car, or neatest home, or biggest boat, or best dressed and behaved children. The list could go on and on.

God gives us our self-worth. He says we are new people, we are adopted children, and we are heirs of God and joint heirs with Christ. We have a mansion waiting for us. What more could we want or need? All the other things pale in comparison to these truths.

Prayer   Lord Jesus, please show us where we find our self-worth, whether it is in You or not. May we be willing to let go of the temporal things and latch onto the eternal truths of who we are. Thank You. Amen

---

My Thoughts

Shortness of Life

Ecclesiastes 3:1-2 There's an opportune time to do things, a right time for everything on the earth: A right time for birth and another for death, A right time to plant and another to reap. (MSG)

My Dad passed on about six years ago now. He had lived a good long life, bloomed where he was planted, left a legacy for his children and grandchildren. There was sadness and grieving and pain, though; my Dad was gone.

Some friends gave me a couple of peony bushes in memory of my father. I bought one to plant in memory of my mother. They both loved springtime. They loved to make plants grow; they loved to watch the garden grow; they thrilled to see flowers blooming. Every spring when my peony plants poke through the ground, I do remember my loving parents.

I am thrilled with the lovely pink and white flowers that bloom. In a very few short weeks, though, the beautiful flowers have wilted and faded—the petals have fallen off. All that is left is the green leaves. And yet, that is beautiful in a different way, as well. I still think of my parents when I see the green foliage, and know that they live on in glory and in my heart.

This spring, my thoughts went another route. I realized how short life is. My Mom lived to be only in her mid-fifties; whereas, my Dad lived to reach eighty-seven – more than thirty years longer than my mother. They both lived life to the fullest and pursued their God-given dreams.

In God's eyes, the difference of thirty years is like a blink of the eye. In comparison to eternity, it is nothing. Like my peony blossoms that last a few short weeks, so is life. Seventy, eighty, ninety or even one hundred years are just a blink of the eye compared to eternity.

Are we preparing for that time when we will be called to eternity to meet our Maker? What can we do to prepare? What will we say when we stand before the God of heaven and earth?

Prayer Oh, God, life is short. As we get a bit older, we realize it anew. Help us, we pray, to keep eternity ever before us, knowing that our time will come to meet You face to face. Please show us the areas that need to be removed in our lives. Help us to submit to those changes and yield to Your working in our lives. We give You the honor and glory and praise. In Jesus' name, we pray. Amen

My Thoughts

Showers

<u>Ezekiel 34:26</u> I'll make them and everything around my hill a blessing. I'll send down plenty of rain in season—showers of blessing! (MSG)

<u>2 Corinthians 1:2</u> May all the gifts and benefits that come from God our Father and the Master, Jesus Christ, be yours! (MSG)

As a young child, we never had running water. Maybe we did—someone would have to run out to the well, and run back to the house with it in a bucket. Mom much preferred rain water for her house plants, though. Often in the winter, Mom would bring in buckets of snow to melt, with which to water her plants. In the summer, she would set out buckets when it was raining to catch as much as possible. Mostly, it was used to water her plants, but there were a few times, she would heat it up on the stove, and we would wash our hair in it.

In our lives, we can put out buckets to catch God's blessing. He is so willing to give it to us, if only we will receive it. He is continually sending blessings to us. Sometimes, we don't see them as blessings. A lot of times, we don't have the buckets set out. There are many uses for those blessings that God gives us. Let's be sure to use them to encourage others, to bless others, to confront others, if need be, to love others, to support others, to comfort others.

> *Prayer O God, how we need You to pour out Your showers of blessing upon us. There are times when You send showers that we don't recognize as blessings. Help us to receive these showers with empty buckets. Pour Your Spirit within us, we pray. Then, may we reach out to bless others with what You have given us. Amen*

My Thoughts

Significance

<u>Psalms 139:14, 17</u> I will praise thee; for I am fearfully and wonderfully made: marvelous are they works; and that my soul knoweth right well. How precious also are thy thoughts unto me, O God! How great is the sum of them. (KJV)

I love playing the piano. I started taking lessons when I was ten years old. In a few short years, I was playing all over the keyboard. It was so much fun.

During this time, I played the old hymns for a few families getting together at home for a church service. After I got married, I then played in a small church for the congregation to sing. As the years rolled by, I played for congregational singing, and often accompanied special vocal selections. I learned how to add runs, trills, and floaties all over the keyboard. It was so cool!

The church we attend now has about one thousand people in attendance. There is a full band playing on stage. I am learning to play the synthesizer. It is quite intimidating. Often I am only playing one little note, or maybe one chord, at a time. It is very hard for me to get used to doing that. The synthesizer is a teeny little part of the whole. Sometimes it seems insignificant, but it does enhance the music. It is a valued instrument in the whole band.

As I thought about this recently, I thought about our lives. In the whole plan of creation, our lives at times, seem quite insignificant. I am one person in a family of nineteen. I am one person in a church of one thousand. I am one person in a city of forty-five thousand. Each of us is just one little person in a world full of millions of people. Yet, God planned for us to be born. He planned who our parents would be. He planned where we would live. He planned the church we would serve in. Let's not forget how important we are to God. We are significant.

Prayer Lord Jesus, thank You for making us exactly like You wanted us to be. Thank You that You have placed us where You want us to be. Help us to constantly remember how much You value us. Help us to remember our lives do enhance others' lives. We are important to You in the whole plan of the universe. Thank You. Amen

---

My Thoughts

Storms

<u>*Ephesians 4:31*</u> Let all bitterness and wrath and anger and clamor and slander be put away from you, along with all malice. (NASB)

In Alberta, we have a saying, "If you don't like the weather, just wait for five minutes." It is true. Our international students are amazed at how quickly our weather changes. It can be bright and sunny one minute and the next, the clouds have rolled in, and before we know it, it is raining. Often those storms are ferocious—rain pouring down in sheets, or hail with a strong wind blowing. It looks devastating with the dark clouds. Often rivers are flowing down the streets. We stand aghast, watching from the window. Then, in the blink of an eye, the sun is shining again, the birds are singing, and all is well. It certainly doesn't take long for the weather to change.

I wonder, with the storms in our lives, how quickly do we change? When the storm is ferocious and long, do we turn to anger, resentment and bitterness? Do the rivers of discouragement, despair, and depression rush into our hearts?

Then, how long will it be before we embrace the Sonshine again? He is just behind the clouds. The clouds will pass. The Son will shine again. Let's cling to the hope of renewed Sonshine in our hearts.

Prayer O Lord Jesus, storms are a part of life. Help us to look beyond the dark clouds, the rain, the hail, the snow, the sleet. When we get bogged down by the storms, help us to turn to You quickly. Amen

---

My Thoughts

Stretching

Luke 22:42 Saying, Father, if thou be willing, remove this cup from me: nevertheless not my will, but thine, be done. (KJVR)

I have watched many guitarists playing, some just by themselves, enjoying their time with the guitar and the music they are playing, others in a band, playing for a group of people to sing. I watch with amazement as they move their fingers from string to string, making the music to flow from the instrument. Each of those strings has to be in tune in order for the right sound to come out of the guitar. Occasionally, I have watched someone tune their guitar. They pick the first string, listen to it, and then either tighten it or loosen it a bit. Once it is satisfactory, they go on to the next one, bending over to listen carefully to make sure it is in tune as well. They continue on with all the strings, then strum a few chords until they are completely satisfied that all is well. The guitar is in the owner's hand, stretching as the owner commands.

I see a likeness between the guitar and our lives. Our Master wants the right tunes to come flowing out of us as well. He bends over us, stretches us here, stretches us there, listening to see if the right melody is coming from deep within. If it isn't the right chord, He continues to stretch us, waiting to see if the new chord, the right chord, will come forth.

What is that right chord that He is longing to hear? I would like to suggest that He wants to hear us whisper, "Not my will, but Thine be done." Then, and only then, will He be satisfied with the music coming from our souls. Let's yield to the Lord's stretching times in our lives.

Prayer _Oh God, so many times we are stretched and stretched, but we don't pay attention to the music that is coming from our souls. We carry on our own merry little way. And yet, that stretching is for a reason. Help us to yield to that stretching and gladly say, "Not my will, but Thine be done." Amen_

My Thoughts

Submit

1 Peter 5:5 Likewise, ye younger, submit yourselves unto the elder. Yea, all of you be subject one to another, and be clothed with humility: for God resisteth the proud, and giveth grace to the humble. (KJV)

Every month, I order a product on line. At first, it was a learning experience to know what to do, what to click on, what not to click on. Each time became easier and easier.

Then one day, the company changed the website. The first time I ordered, I did okay. The product arrived a few days later. The next month, I ordered again, and the product never did come. So I went onto the site to see what was what. It never showed that I had ordered anything at all that month. So I ordered again. Once more, the product never came.

I was frustrated, so I called a friend to help me through this process. I had done everything right, except the very last step. Away down at the bottom of the page, there was a button that said, "Submit". I needed to click on that button. As soon as I did that, the order was sent, and the product arrived a few days later. As my friend was helping me through this, and I realized I hadn't clicked on "submit", I told her that there could be a spiritual lesson in this.

Psalms 18:30 God--His way is perfect; the word of the LORD is pure. He is a shield to all who take refuge in Him. (HCSB)

Romans 8:27-28 He knows us far better than we know ourselves, knows our pregnant condition, and keeps us present before God. That's why we can be so sure that every detail in our lives of love for God is worked into something good. (MSG)

Let's submit first of all to the Lord. His way is perfect. We can trust Him. He is our shield. He knows us far better than we know ourselves. He knows every detail of our lives, and He promises to work those details into something good. Submitting to others requires humility. God will give grace to the humble. Oh, how we need His grace!

Prayer Lord Jesus, we think we know ourselves pretty good, but You know us better than we know ourselves. We like to live in denial sometimes and not face reality. We can't hide from You, though. Help us to be open and honest with you. That is submitting to you, and that requires humility as well. Help us to be open and honest with others. Help us to trust You in every detail of our lives. Help us to claim Your promise that You will work every detail in our lives for You into something good. Often we don't see how that is possible, but Your Word is true—You cannot lie. We need You today. We give You the praise and honor and glory for all that You do in our lives. Thank You. Amen

My Thoughts

Team Work

Acts 27:3 Julius was very kind to Paul and let him go ashore to visit with friends so they could provide for his needs. (NLT)

Proverbs 14:20 The rich have many friends. (NLT)

I am a pretty independent person. I have seen that many times in my life. How I've noticed this recently is in playing the piano at church. Years ago in churches, the piano was the only instrument. For years I played the piano in church, both for congregational singing and in accompanying special vocal contributions. The song leader was supposed to set the tempo, and I was to follow that. Most of the time, though, the leader wouldn't lead, so I would unconsciously take over and set the tempo. With only one instrument, it was me who was the musician. I didn't have to work with anyone (except the song leader who wouldn't lead) to co-ordinate the sounds. There was no input. It was an individual effort, and could get lonely.

Now the church we attend is huge. I am learning to play the synthesizer, as part of a band. The drummer is the one who sets the tempo, and the rest of us follow that. We have built relationships with each other in order to produce good music from the band. We are really a small group—supporting one another, making suggestions, adjusting to benefit the whole.

God made us for relationships. We need them. We need accountability. We need input into our lives from trusted individuals. We were not made to live independently. Let's remember that we need others in our lives to help us grow. Let's purposefully build our relationships. That is what God wants. Life is pretty lonely without meaningful relationships. Of course, our first and foremost relationship is to be with Jesus Christ. Then it is to be with others.

Prayer Dear Lord Jesus, so many times we go off on our own and try to do life independently. That can be very lonely. Thank You that You created us for healthy relationships. Help us to nurture those relationships where others will support us, speak truth into our souls, and accept us exactly like we are. Thank You that You are a God of relationships. Amen

---

My Thoughts

The Pilot

Isaiah 40:31 But those who hope in the Lord will renew their strength. They will soar on wings like eagles; they will run and not grow weary, they will walk and not be faint. (NIV)

I was going on a flight recently. Before I left, it was stormy – snowing and blowing, in fact. I am always a little apprehensive about flying, so the weather didn't help that. The take-off was uneventful: the whole flight was uneventful except that as we were going up through the storm clouds, the going got pretty rough. My apprehension arose. But within a few minutes, we had risen above those storm clouds. It was no longer rough and the sun was shining brightly. I could look down and see the clouds, and they were beautiful – soft billowy clouds like pillows, where a person could just lie down and rest in complete contentment.

Then, my thoughts turned to the experiences of life. So many times, we are in the midst of a storm. It is cold and miserable, and the wind is blowing fiercely. We long to be in the bright sunlight again where it is peaceful and beautiful. I've discovered that the way to that bright sunlight often entails going through some real bumpy times – like up through the clouds in that aircraft. It gets pretty rough. There is a storm before the calm. We have to trust the Pilot, and let Him take us up and beyond. Then, and only then, will the "Sonlight" flood our souls. We are at peace. We can rest in the soft pillows. We can look at those clouds and storms as a learning and growing time.

There are times, though, when the storm lasts a long time. And there are times when the band of clouds is very thick, and it takes a long time to get through it. We get weary and anxious. But the outcome is always the same – if we trust the Pilot. There is "Sonlight" on the other side.

Hebrews 13:5 God has said, "Never will I leave you; never will I forsake you." (NIV)

> *Prayer Lord Jesus, we pray that we will rest completely, and trust You completely in the storms of life, knowing that these storms are for a reason—to make us more like You. Our hearts' desire is to be more like You, but we don't like the storms. Help us to keep our eyes on You, the "Sonlight", then soar like the eagles and rise above the situations. Amen*

My Thoughts

Thunder

<u>John 14:27</u> Peace I leave with you; My peace I give to you; not as the world gives do I give to you. Do not let your heart be troubled, nor let it be fearful. (NASB)

During the summer, we have ferocious thunder storms. Often, these storms are in the middle of the night. The thunder wakes me up, and I lie awake until the storm passes.

My Dad, on the other hand, would sleep his best during a thunder storm. When he was visiting us quite a few years ago, I asked him if he had heard the thunder during the night. It had been very loud. He hadn't heard a thing, and slept like a baby.

I saw in my Dad such a complete trust in God in every situation in his life. Such strength he had in the adverse events of his life. I'm sure this is why he had complete peace and rest in the storms. Only Jesus can give us that peace. He has promised it to us as seen in today's Scripture verse. Are we claiming it as ours? Or are we letting that gift lay by the wayside, unused?

Prayer   Lord Jesus, You promised to give us Your peace. Help us to claim that promise when life is going good, and when the storms hit. Amen

---

My Thoughts

To Fix or Not to Fix

Galatians 6:2 Share each other's troubles and problems, and in this way obey the law of Christ. (NLT)

One of my clients has a couple of finches. They are such tiny little birds. I had never seen such little birds up close before. But there was something even smaller in the cage. There were about six teeny little eggs in the nest. I couldn't believe the size of them. I could hardly wait until they hatched, and I could see those teeny little birds. The next time I was there, the eggs were gone—but there were no baby finches either.

I was told the eggs did hatch and the young were doing fine until the male finch tried to fix the nest for the mother and her babies. In doing that, he fluffed things up in the nest, and added more "comfortable stuff" to make it better for the babies. The problem, though, was that in doing this, the babies were smothered.

How often we try to "fix" things for others. So many times, we "smother" those we're trying to fix. We add too much "comfortable stuff" in their lives. We often enable them to carry on in their dysfunctional ways. There is a difference between "fixing" and legitimately helping others. Fixing is not helping them to see their own issues that need to be dealt with. Supporting and encouraging is helping them to see what they need to do in order to grow. If the finch had "helped" with the young, they would have grown to healthy adults. But "fixing" destroyed them. May it be our goal to help others to grow to maturity— and at the same time, not to fix them. We all need to see that we are responsible for our own actions. If we don't allow others to take responsibility for their actions, it doesn't help them one little bit.

Galatians 6:5 For we are each responsible for our own conduct. (NLT)

Prayer _Lord Jesus, we see so many needy, hurting people in our world. They need help. We know their healing comes from You alone. We are told, though, to share their troubles and problems. Please show us where we can be an encouragement and bear the burdens you want us to, but also show us, if we do bear the burdens that they need to, where we are fixing and smothering instead of offering help. Grant us to be ever sensitive to Your leading. Amen_

My Thoughts

Traditions

<u>*Deuteronomy 11:18-19*</u>   Place these words on your hearts. Get them deep inside you. Tie them on your hands and foreheads as a reminder. Teach them to your children. Talk about them wherever you are, sitting at home or walking in the street; talk about them from the time you get up in the morning until you fall into bed at night. (MSG)

As Easter approaches, I am looking forward to preparing Easter dinner for my family. I will put a ham in the oven to cook. I will peal a whole pot of potatoes and make a yummy six-layer dessert. I will hide Easter eggs for the children. Similarly, at Christmas time, I always put a turkey in to cook, peal the same pot of potatoes, and have Christmas baking for dessert. I make sure the gifts are under the tree before the family arrives. We have traditions. They are important to our family.

Each family has their own traditions—Christmas traditions, Thanksgiving traditions, vacation traditions, meal traditions, weekend traditions. Every family's traditions are unique. Even as we talk about our individual family traditions, I think children feel more secure because of them.

God talks about traditions in today's Scripture verses as well. Oh, how he wants us to pass on to our children and grandchildren the traditions of sharing His love and faithfulness by word and deed.

Prayer   Lord Jesus, traditions are important. It is important to speak to our families about You and Your Word, sharing Your faithfulness to all generations. Help us in this area. Amen

---

My Thoughts

Traffic

Psalms 18:2 The LORD is my rock, and my fortress, and my deliverer; my God, my strength, in whom I will trust; my buckler, and the horn of my salvation, and my high towers. (KJVR)

Galatians 5:1 Christ has set us free to live a free life. So take your stand! (MSG)

One day as I was going for a walk, I was amazed to see a medium-sized dog cross the street. It was a very busy street. He stood and watched for a while. Then he went across one lane of traffic, and stood and waited for the next lane to clear so he could go those few extra feet to the next lane. I stood in awe as I watched him go completely across the six lane street safely to the other side. I wondered if he was filled with fear. He looked very confident. I assume he had done this many times before, and had built up the confidence to continue crossing busy streets. What about the first time though? It was likely very scary. After repeating this procedure many times, he had the confidence to continue. Yes, he was cautious, and maybe he was scared, but he didn't let that stop him.

I thought about us as we go through life. Sometimes, we are faced with crossing traffic that is seemingly unsafe. When we go against the flow of our ingrained behaviors, it can be scary. These behaviors could be addictions of any kind—approval addictions, or drug addictions, or control addictions. We know we need to step out from them and change our behavior, but it is too hard. We try to do it on our own, but fail miserably. We can only rely on Jesus Christ and His power to continually make the right choice.

2 Timothy 1:7 For God hath not given us the spirit of fear; but of power, and of love, and of a sound mind. (KJVR)

As we take the first step across a busy road to get to where we want to be, where we need to be, let's remember to completely depend on the Lord. He has not given us the spirit of fear.

Prayer Lord Jesus, life can be very scary. We know, at times, we need to make changes to bring glory and honor to Your Name, but we can't do it ourselves. In order to be free, we have to step out to make those changes, while clinging to You the whole time. Help us, we pray. Amen

My Thoughts

Trusting

<u>1 Corinthians 10:13</u> There hath no temptation taken you but such as is common to man: but God is faithful, who will not suffer you to be tempted above that ye are able; but will with the temptation also make a way to escape, that ye may be able to bear it. (KJV)

One day as I was going for a walk, I had to stand at a busy intersection, and wait for the traffic to clear, and the light to turn. The intersection is at the highway leading through town, so there is a lot of heavy, big traffic passing by. One of our main industries here is lumber, so there are many log- hauling trucks on the roads.

As I was standing there waiting, a big rig hauling logs turned from going east to going north. As he passed by within a few feet of me, anxiety filled my heart briefly. I thought that if that load of logs happened to come off, they would all land on top of me, and that would be the end. Just as quickly as that anxiety reached my heart, the truth came to me that I had to trust that the driver knew how many logs he could haul safely, and had secured the load properly.

In our Christian lives, we are to trust the driver as well--that driver is Jesus Christ. We are to trust that He knows what is best for us and how much we can carry. We may be apprehensive and fearful when we take a deep look at life and what is before us. But God is trustworthy.

> *Prayer Thank You, God, that You are trustworthy and that You are faithful. Help us to trust You with every detail of our lives, both when the load is heavy and when the load is light. Amen*

My Thoughts

Tunnels

1 Kings 12:24 "For this thing has come from Me." (NASB)

Matthew 19:26 With God all things are possible. (NASB)

Recently, I was struggling with life. I was overwhelmed with the things that were happening to me. All I could see was darkness. There seemed to be no light at the end of the tunnel. In fact, the tunnel was way too long, way too dark, way too crooked.

Then one day, I read in my devotions the Scripture for today. "This thing is from Me," God told me. I couldn't understand that. Why would these struggles be from Him? He continued to work in my heart. I finally accepted the truth that He was allowing these things in my life at this time for a reason. When I admitted that, the tunnel wasn't quite as dark, nor was it quite as long, nor so crooked. Then God, in His love, assured me that all things are possible with Him. At that moment, I knew that in my head but not in my heart. I wrestled with God for a while over that truth as well, but finally rested on it. Did the circumstances change immediately? No, but peace had returned to my soul, and I knew God was directing me down this dark path at the time.

Psalms 142:3 When my spirit was overwhelmed within me, then thou knewest my path. (KJVR)

Psalms 119:105 Thy word is a lamp unto my feet, and a light unto my path. (KJVR)

We don't like the dark tunnels, the crooked paths that we are on. Let's claim the truths of God's Word and allow Him to guide us. He knows the path already. He is so willing to shine the light of His Word for us, if only we will claim those truths as ours.

> *Prayer Lord Jesus, Your Word is true. Often we don't want to believe it. We can't understand why we are in the tunnels. Help us to trust Your leading in the crooked, hard paths of life. We praise You for Your wisdom. Without the tunnels, we wouldn't learn some of the things You want to teach us. Help us, we pray. Amen*

My Thoughts

Underlying

Psalms 139:23-24 Investigate my life, O God, find out everything about me; Cross-examine and test me, get a clear picture of what I'm about; See for yourself whether I've done anything wrong—then guide me on the road to eternal life. (MSG)

I have had a stiff arm for the past few months. I have been going to a chiropractor who is specialized in a certain type of treatment called Active Release Techniques. This provides a way to diagnose and treat the underlying cause of my problem. I like that concept. Just a surface solution isn't really any solution at all. This type of treatment is very painful. I have to trust the chiropractor when each muscle hurts terribly as she is working on it. After a few weeks of this treatment, it does feel better, the movement has improved, and the pain is pretty well gone.

I see this happening in our lives so often. We have some pain deep down in our souls. We want a quick fix. We don't want to go through the hard work of releasing the pain. We think if we just fix the surface problems that all will be well. How mistaken we are! The problem is still there. It doesn't go away without some active release techniques used on them.

What do those techniques look like in our lives? It means breaking the denial by vocalizing our pain to a trusted friend. It means grieving over the loss of something in our lives. Even if the expectation was unrealistic, it has caused pain and we need to accept that fact. It means claiming God's promises. It means finding a church or small group that shows God's grace. It is here we can be candid and still be accepted.

Let's look at the causes of our current behaviors. Let's ask God to show us what is really going on down in our souls. Let's ask Him to show us where we have been wounded and need healing. He wants to heal us more than we want it ourselves.

> *Prayer Lord Jesus, so many times we go about our lives glibly, not always realizing something is amiss in our souls. And if we do, we often don't want to look at it. It is far too painful. Investigate our lives, O God. Thank You that You will not abandon us as orphans. You promise to come to us (John 14:18 NLT) Help us to be brutally honest with ourselves and to trust You through this process. Thank You. Amen*

My Thoughts

My Thoughts

Value in Letters

Psalms 119:15-16 I ponder every morsel of wisdom from you, I attentively watch how you've done it. I relish everything you've told me of life, I won't forget a word of it. (MSG)

My Mom was the best letter writer I have known. I never really knew that until I moved away from home as a teen-ager. She would write weekly. Sometimes, the letters were long. Sometimes they were short. She would go into great detail about the daily events on the farm, the news from the extended family, and the neighbourhood news. The way she had of describing things and situations was amazing. I would look forward to receiving a letter from her every week.

After my Mom passed away, my Dad took up the ritual of letter writing to me every week. His letters were different. He included all the news of family and friends, but not much detail or description. His letters consisted of one page of paper written on both sides. He never enjoyed it like my Mom did, but bless his heart, he wrote every week as well, filling me in on all the news.

I have a few of the last letters that Mom wrote—also my Dad's last few letters. Sometimes I read them. A host of emotions run through me. I feel sad that they are both gone now, and I miss them and their love for me and their prayers for me. Sometimes I laugh because of something funny they have told me. Sometimes I weep. I am so glad that I have kept these letters. They are very precious to me. I will cherish them all of my life.

You know, God's Word is His letter to us. Do we read it? How often do we read it? Does it bring sadness? Laughter? Weeping? Do we cherish it like we should? Is it precious to us? Do we ponder it? Let's consider these questions today.

Mark 13:31 Heaven and earth will pass away, but My words will not pass away. (NASB)

Prayer Lord Jesus, we take so many things for granted—things like our parent's love for us, their life, Your love for us, Your Word that You gave us. Our parents pass on to glory. We miss them deeply. Thank You that your Word will never pass away. Help us to relish it and ponder it and apply it to our lives. Speak to us today, we pray. Amen

My Thoughts

What a Feast!

Jeremiah 15:16 When your words showed up, I ate them—swallowed them whole. What a feast! What delight I took in being yours, O GOD, GOD-of-the-Angel-Armies! (MSG)

I know a few families who have horses. Often, the horses are in a pasture very close to the house. I have seen these people run out to rub their horse when they get home. Sometimes, they take an apple or carrot to feed their horse. Of course, the horse looks forward to it, whinnying when the family arrives home. He is waiting anxiously for his treat of the day. The family loves their horses, and wants to give them treats to let them know they are loved.

God loves us and wants us to know that, too. He offers us food to eat. It can come in the form of Bible reading, attending church, and listening to the messages, or small group studies and interaction. Often, His food comes in ways that we don't always recognize. There are times it could come in the form of a friend's words of wisdom to us. It can come in the form of being confronted by a close friend. It could come in a beautiful sunset we see, or birds singing or flying. It could be in the form of a baby, or little children, or the aged grandparent.

Are we ready and willing to eat what God offers us? Do we see the food He offers us?

Open our Eyes, Lord, by Bob Cull, is so meaningful.

> Open our eyes, Lord,
> We want to see Jesus;
> To reach out and touch Him
> And say that we love Him.
> Open our ears, Lord,
> And help us to listen,
> Open our eyes, Lord,
> We want to see Jesus.

Prayer Oh Lord, we do love You. Open our eyes, we want to see You. We want to touch You. We want to hear from You. We can do these things by feeding on Your Word, in whatever way it comes to us. Help us, we pray. In Jesus' Name. Amen

---

My Thoughts

What Does the Lord See?

<u>2 Chronicles 16:9</u> "For the eyes of the LORD move to and fro throughout the earth that He may strongly support those whose heart is completely His." (NASB)

My Dad has been gone a few years now. I have thought a lot about his life since his passing on.

Because he was born in 1913, one thing he saw a lot of was change. In the farming industry alone, he saw small farms, the fields ploughed with a horse and a one bottom plough. Then, he saw small ten horsepower tractors with small five-foot cultivators, and on up to huge five hundred horsepower tractors with sixty-foot deep tillage cultivators. He saw the harvesting change from stooks and threshing machines to combines and tractors and trucks. Transportation changed from walking, or riding a horse, to trains, to cars, to airplanes, to rockets. Running water and indoor plumbing was another change. Ways of communication changed hugely in those ninety some years. How exciting it was when the phones, radios and televisions were brought in. When Dad was visiting once, he was amazed that I could email my siblings, and it would be in their computer with a simple click of the finger.

God also sees many changes as He looks down from heaven. He sees the physical things that we see—in fact, He knew they would be invented before time began. He sees deeper than that though. He sees into our hearts. He is alert and constantly on the look out for those who are totally committed to Him. Oh, how His heart must ache when He sees unbelief, discord, resentment, bitterness, hatred and dishonesty.

Let's be aware of His eyes--always searching, always on the alert, looking.

Prayer Lord Jesus, how things change—from decade to decade, from year to year, from day to day, from hour to hour. Some change is good; some is bad. We do know that change is inevitable. May we be responsive to Your prodding, and be willing to change to bring honour and glory to Your name. Amen

My Thoughts

What's Next, Papa?

2 Timothy 1:7 God's Spirit doesn't make cowards out of us. The Spirit gives us power, love, and self-control. (CEV)

Last summer, we were having a neighborhood barbecue in our back yard. The weather was cool, and it started to rain. We had finished eating, but some of us wanted to visit some more. We decided to carry a few things downstairs, and continue visiting where it was out of the wind and rain, where it was warm.

On the way downstairs, I slipped and fell, landing on my back, part way down. I just lay and moaned and groaned for a while. When I went to stand up, the pain was excruciating. How it hurt to move! Once seated, I was okay shortly thereafter. Then again, when I went to get up, the pain was unbearable. Each time I would sit or lie still, I would be fine, but the moving of my position was what hurt. Walking hurt, turning hurt, bending hurt. I was afraid to move because I hurt so badly. After visiting my doctor, I found that nothing was broken. It would only take time to heal and for the pain to disappear. Even now at times, I have pain in that part of my back—a reminder that I was hurt there.

I could have been filled with fear of ever going down steps again. But I wasn't. I wish I could say that about my spiritual journey. So many times, I fall flat on my face. Yes, it hurts. It hurts to try to get up. It hurts to move in any direction. It just plain hurts. I am afraid to try again. Will I fall again? Will I be hurt again? How badly will I be hurt the next time? Will I recover? How long will the recovery take? Do I even want to recover? Or do I want to stay where I'm at? If I do recover, am I going to hurt in that same spot again? A lot of good questions to ask!

Romans 8:15 This resurrection life you received from God is not a timid, grave-tending life. It's adventurously expectant, greeting God with a childlike "What's next, Papa?" (MSG)

As children of the King, we are not cowards, nor are we timid. We have power to get up, get moving again, and heal in the process. Life is an adventure. God is our Papa. He cares for us and wants us to keep moving forward.

My Thoughts

Where Are We Going?

Daniel 1:8 Daniel purposed in his heart . . . (KJV)

We live in a small city that is growing rapidly. There didn't use to be a rush hour in the morning and afternoon. It was kind of a sleepy little city. As it has grown, though, there are rush hours now.

I really noticed that the other morning on my way to work. All of us were intent in getting to work. We had a purpose. Each of us had a different destination, but we did know where we were going. Each of us had a different route to go on, but again, we knew where we were going.

I thought about that in reference to our individual, private lives. First and foremost, we need to accept Jesus as Lord and Savior. That will ensure that we go to heaven.

But then what? What is our purpose after that? Do we know what our purpose is, or are we floundering around trying to find meaning to life? Do we know where we are going?

In the deep recesses of our souls, we know that our purpose is to serve God. Every one of us has a different route to go on to do that. There are manual laborers and professionals; there are housewives and mothers; there are pastors and teachers; there are doctors and nurses. The list could go on and on. We can all be serving the Lord with our professions, and thereby have a purpose and meaning to our lives. I would like to suggest that we need to check our motives often to see if we're serving God and others, or if we are serving ourselves.

Matthew 4:10 Thou shalt worship the Lord your God and Him only shalt thou serve. (KJV)

Prayer Father in Heaven, how easy it is to get wrapped up in meaningless things in life. Help us to keep You front and foremost in our minds so that we are serving You at all times. Help us to be a blessing to someone today. Amen

---

My Thoughts

Which Battery?

Mark 12:30 And you must love the Lord your God with all your heart, all your soul, all your mind, and all your strength. (NLT)

Occasionally, I buy for one of my grandchildren a gift that requires batteries. Then, of course, I have to buy the right size of battery to make the toy work. I am careful to read on the box what size it needs and how many it needs. If it needs three AAA batteries, that is what I buy. That is what charges up the toy and makes it work.

If I had a toy that needed a single C battery, the little AAA batteries wouldn't connect to the needed points, even if I tried to cram three of them into the battery compartment. One would think a large D battery would do better because it has more capacity. But no, it doesn't work either.

I thought about our lives in relation to these batteries. Christ Jesus could be likened to a battery that fits the exact shape of the empty compartment in our lives. He is the only One Who will fit there, charge us up, and make our lives work properly.

Isaiah 44:6 I am the First and the Last; there is no other God. (NLT)

Prayer Lord Jesus, help us to be aware of the batteries we try to stick into our lives. Help us to always put you first, for You are the only One who can give us the power we need to live every day, one day at a time. Amen

---

My Thoughts

Winter All Year?

<u>Ecclesiastes 3:1</u> Everything has its own time, and there is a specific time for every activity under heaven: (GW)

<u>Ecclesiastes 3:11</u> It is beautiful how God has done everything at the right time. (GW)

In northern Alberta, Canada, we had an unusually long winter this past year. From the first snow fall until it was all melted was six long months. In March, one of my little grandsons said wearily, "I think winter is going to last all year long this year." So we talked about how God has specific seasons for us: winter, spring, summer and autumn. One thing we do know is that spring will come—we just don't know when.

In our lives, we have seasons as well. We love the spring times and the summer times. Things are going great. We are growing. Life is good. Then come the autumn times in our lives. Often, we feel discouraged. We have winter times in our lives, as well. We see no hope, no light at the end of the tunnel at all. We feel depressed. I have learned not to fight the winter times in my life. Winter is a season. It will pass. Spring time will come again. We don't know when, but God is faithful. There are specific times for every activity here on earth. Jesus will never leave us nor forsake us—in any season of our lives.

<u>Hebrews 13:5</u> Let your conversation be without covetousness; and be content with such things as ye have: for he hath said, I will never leave thee, nor forsake thee. (KJV)

Prayer God in heaven, we thank You that there is a purpose and a time for everything that happens. We also thank You, Lord Jesus, that You will never leave us nor forsake us, in any season of our lives. Help us to trust You at all times. Amen

---

My Thoughts

Wounds and Truth

<u>Proverbs 27:6</u> Faithful are the wounds of a friend, But deceitful are the kisses of an enemy. (NASB)

I love playing the piano. I love finding a hard piece of music to practice. I love adding frills in order to make the music sound like I want it to. I love slowing down, and speeding up, and playing louder, and playing softer to give the song expression.

That isn't the way I used to play the piano, though. I used to just pound. Whatever song I chose to play, it had to be played hard, and loud, and fast! Often, I took my frustrations, or my hurts, or my pain out on the piano. Those listening could tell that.

One day, my Mom (bless her heart) told me that I just pounded the piano, and I didn't use any expression. That was during a time I was practicing a hard arrangement of "In the Sweet Bye and Bye". It was very difficult. I spent hours practicing. But like my Mom said, there was no expression; it all sounded loud and fast. You couldn't tell there was a "Sweet Bye and Bye".

I remember those words of Mom's as if she said them yesterday. I am so glad that she had the courage to tell me the truth. Like the Scripture verse for today—faithful are the wounds of a friend. Yes, it hurt when she told me, but I took it to heart. Over the years, I have learned to play with expression. I believe it began when mom planted that seed of truth in my mind. The truth does set us free.

<u>John 8:32</u> Then you will experience for yourselves the truth, and the truth will free you." (MSG)

Most of us have people who can speak truth into our lives. They don't do it to hurt us, although it may hurt. They do it to encourage us, to help us see an area in our lives that needs some attention, to set us free in the long run. Oh, may we listen and let the truths sink deep into our souls.

Prayer Father, we have all been hurt at times by what others say to us. Sometimes, people do say things intentionally to hurt us; but other times, our closest family and friends, who love us so much, speak truth to us. Often we don't want to hear it. Lord, I pray that You will help us to sift the intentional hurts, and the hurts done in love. Help us to forgive where needed. We do want to grow and change. This is one way we can do that, if we are willing to look at truth. Oh, how we need You today. Amen

My Thoughts

You are What You Do!

<u>Ephesians 1:5</u> God had already decided that through Jesus Christ he would make us his children---this was his pleasure and purpose. (GNB)

At the gym where I exercise, there is a white board where inspiring messages are written. One of those messages recently read, "You are what you do!" It meant if we exercise and eat properly, we will be healthy and have more energy.

In the spiritual realm, we are what we do with Jesus, because of what Jesus Christ has done for us. Yes, Jesus willingly came to earth to die for all of us—everyone who has ever lived, everyone who is living now and everyone who will live in the future. He offers all of us the free gift of eternal life.

<u>Romans 6:23</u> For sin pays its wage---death; but God's free gift is eternal life in union with Christ Jesus our Lord. (GNB)

It is our choice to accept that gift or reject it. Choosing to accept Jesus Christ as our Saviour guarantees a place in heaven for us eternally. The choice to accept that gift sets us free. By accepting Jesus, we become children of the King. It is all because of Him.

I love the chorus to the song, *A Child of the King*, by Harriet E. Buell—

> I'm a child of the King,
> A child of the King:
> With Jesus my Saviour,
> I'm a child of the King.

Let's remember that it is true: we are what we are because of the choice we have made.

Prayer Thank You, Jesus, for what You did for us that we couldn't possibly do for ourselves. Thank You for offering us eternal life. It doesn't end there though. You keep changing us and growing us all through our lives. Help us to yield to that change. That is a choice as well. If we choose to yield, we will become more like Jesus every day. We love You. Amen

---

My Thoughts

Expiry Date

John 3:16 For God so greatly loved and dearly prized the world that He (even) gave up His only begotten (unique) Son, so that whoever believes in (trusts in, clings to, relies on) Him shall not perish (come to destruction, be lost) but have eternal (everlasting) life. (AMP)

I am really annoyed with myself. This afternoon I have to throw out fifteen dollars. (Even Canadian currency, this is a substantial amount!) Oh, that was not my original intention. At first, I planned to save money. I carefully clipped and saved some special coupons for various useful grocery products.

The not-saving part came when I stuck them in my wallet and forgot about them. Today, while cleaning out my purse, I came across my "bargains" – with their expiry dates past. What a waste!

God has given us a coupon for eternal life and forgiveness in Jesus. All we have to do is take it and put it in our heart. God's Son, Jesus, died on the cross for our sin. He was raised from the dead, just because of God's love for us.

Unfortunately, not all of us use our coupon. Some will toss it, believing that their sins are so terrible that God won't be able to forgive. Others will choose to set aside God's free offer after hearing about it. They want to pay for a debt themselves that has already been paid in full. Still others choose to believe that God can't possibly love them enough to let them use the coupon. But the expiry date on our coupon is the date of our death. We don't get a second chance after that, and none of us knows when that day is.

What a blessing that so many have taken God at His Word and have used the coupon of Jesus' sacrifice to enter God's rest and to look forward to eternal life. How will each of us use God's coupon?

Prayer Thanks, God, that Your coupon has not yet expired. Lord, we want to know You in the fullness of Your Son, Jesus Christ. We are tired of putting off the truth of Your love. We choose Jesus now. Help us to understand who He is. Make Him real in our hearts. Amen

---

Song List

And

Lyrics

Song List

1. All Heaven Declares

All heav'n declares the glory of the risen Lord.
Who can compare with the beauty of the Lord.
Forever He will be the Lamb upon the throne.
I gladly bow the knee and worship Him alone.

I will proclaim the glory of the risen Lord.
Who once was slain to reconcile man to God.
Forever You will be the Lamb upon the throne.
I gladly bow the knee and worship Him alone.

2. Come, Now is the Time to Worship

Come, now is the time to worship,
Come, now is the time to give your heart,
Come, just as you are to worship,
Come, just as you are before your God.
Come.
One day every tongue will confess you are God.
One day every knee will bow.
Still the greatest treasure remains for those
Who gladly choose you now.

3. Open Our Eyes

Open our eyes, Lord, we want to see Jesus;
To reach out and touch Him and say that we love Him.
Open our ears, Lord, and help us to listen.
Open our eyes, Lord, we want to see Jesus.

4. I Believe in Jesus

I believe in Jesus, I believe He is the Son of God,
I believe He died and rose again,
I believe He paid for us all.
And I believe He's here now, standing in our midst.
Here with the power to heal now, and the grace to forgive.

5. He is Lord

He is Lord! He is Lord!
He is risen form the dead and He is Lord.
Ev'ry knee shall bow, ev'ry tongue confess
That Jesus Christ is Lord!

6. Oh, How He Loves and Me

Oh, how He loves you and me;
Oh, how He loves you and me.
 He gave His life—what more could He give?
Oh, how He loves you; Oh, how He loves me;
Oh, how He loves you and me.

Jesus to Calv'ry did go,
His love for sinners to show.
What He did there brought hope from despair.
Oh, how He loves you;
Oh, how He loves me;
Oh, how He loves you and me.

7. Jesus, Name Above All Names

Jesus, name above all names,
Beautiful Savior, glorious Lord.
Emmanuel: God is with us!
Blessed Redeemer, Living Word.

8. I Exalt Thee

For Thou, O Lord, art high above all the earth;
Thou art exalted far above all gods.
For Thou, O Lord, art high above all the earth;
Thou art exalted far above all gods.
I exalt Thee, I exalt Thee, I exalt Thee, O Lord.
I exalt Thee, I exalt Thee, I exalt Thee, O Lord.

9. Thou Art Worthy

Thou art worthy, Thou art worthy,
Thou art worthy, O Lord.
To receive glory, glory and honor,
Glory and honor and power.
For Thou hast created, hast all things created;
Thou hast created all things,
And for Thy pleasure they are created,
For Thou art worthy, O Lord.

10. Supper Time

Many years ago in days of childhood
I used to play till evening shadows come,
Then winding down an old familiar pathway
I heard my mother call at set of sun.

Come home, come home, it's supper time,
The shadows lengthen fast;
Come home, come home, it's supper time;
We're going home at last.

One day beside her bedside I was kneeling,
And angle wings were winnowing the air;
She heard the call for supper time in heaven,
And now I know she's waiting for me there.

In visions now I see her standing yonder,
And her familiar voice I hear once more;
The banquet table's ready up in heaven,
It's supper time upon the golden shore.

11. Seek Ye First

Seek ye first the kingdom of God
And His righteousness;
And all these things shall be added unto you.
Hallelu, hallelujah.

Where two or three are gathered in my name.
There am I in their midst.
And what soever ye shall ask, I will do.
Hallelu, hallelujah.

12. Create in Me a Clean Heart

Create in me a clean heart, O God,
And renew a right spirit within me.
Create in me a clean heart, O God,
And renew a right spirit within me.

Cast me not away from They presence, O Lord,
And take not Thy Holy Spirit from me.
Restore unto me the joy of They salvation,
And renew a right spirit within me.

13. Spirit of the Living God

Spirit of the living God, Fall fresh on me.
Spirit of the living God, Fall fresh on me.
Melt me, mold me, fill me, use me.
Spirit of the living God, Fall fresh on me.

14. He's Still Workin' on Me/Little by Little

He's still workin' on me
To make me what I ought to be;
It took Him just a week to make the moon and stars,
The sun and the earth and Jupiter and Mars.
How loving and patient He must be!
He's still workin' on me!

Little by little He's changing me,
Line after line until I can see,
Precept on precept until I am free;
Jesus is changing me.

He's still workin' on me
To make me what I ought to be;
It took Him just a week to make the moon and stars,
The sun and the earth and Jupiter and Mars.
How loving and patient He must be!
He's still workin' on me!

15. Faithful One

Faithful One, so unchanging,
Ageless One, You're my rock of peace.
Lord of all, I depend on You,
I call out to You, again and again,
I call out to You, again and again.
You are my rock in times of trouble,
You lift me up when I fall down.
All though the storm, Your love is the anchor,
My hope is in You alone.

16. I Will Serve Thee

I will serve Thee because I love Thee;
You have given life to me.
I was nothing before You found me;
You have given life to me.
Heart aches, broken pieces,
Ruined lives are shy You died on Calvary.
Your touch was what I longed for;
You have given life to me.

17. Jesus is Lord of All

All my tomorrow, all my past;
Jesus is Lord of all.
I've quit my struggles, contentment at last;
Jesus is Lord of all.

King of kinds, Lord of lords;
Jesus is Lord of all.
All my possessions and all my life.
Jesus is Lord of all.
All of my conflicts, all my thoughts;
Jesus is Lord of all.
His love wins the battles I could not have fought;
Jesus is Lord of all.

18. Something Beautiful

Something beautiful, something good;
All my confusion He understood.
All I had to offer Him was brokenness and strife,
But He made something beautiful of my life.

19. Follow Me

I traveled down a lonely road
And no one seemed to care,
The burden on my weary back
Had bowed me to despair;
I oft complained to Jesus
How folds were treating me,
And then I heard Him say so tenderly:
My feet were also weary
Upon the Calv'ry road,
The cross became so heavy,
I fell beneath the load;
Be faithful, weary pilgrim,
The morning I can see—
Just lift your cross and follow close to me.

20. The Joy of the Lord

The joy of the Lord is my strength;
The joy of the Lord is my strength;
The joy of the Lord is my strength;
The joy of the Lord is my strength.

He gives me living water and I thirst no more;
He gives me living water and I thirst no more;
He gives me living water and I thirst no more;
The joy of the Lord is my strength.

If you want joy, you must praise for it;
If you want joy, you must praise for it;
If you want joy, you must praise for it;
The joy of the Lord is my strength.

21. This is the Day/Thy Loving Kindness

This is the day, this is the day
That the Lord has made, that they Lord has made.
We will rejoice, we will rejoice
And be glad in it, and be glad in nit.
This is the day that the Lord has made;
We will rejoice and be glad in it.
This is the day, this is the day
That the Lord has made.

Thy loving kindness is better than life.
Thy loving kindness is better than life.
My lips shall praise Thee, thus will I bless Thee
I will lift up my hands unto Thy Name.

I lift my hands, Lord, unto Thy Name.
I lift my hands, Lord, unto Thy Name.
My lips shall praise Thee, thus will I bless Thee
I will lift up my hands unto Thy Name.

22. The Longer I Serve Him

Since I started for the Kingdom,
Since my life He controls,
Since I gave my heart to Jesus,
The longer I serve Him,
The sweeter He grows.

The longer I serve Him the sweeter He grows,
The more that I love Him, more love He bestows;
Each day is like heaven, my heart overflows,
The longer I serve Him the sweeter He grows.

Every need He is supplying,
Plenteous grace He bestows;
Every day my way gets brighter,
The longer I serve Him, the sweeter He grows.

The longer I serve Him the sweeter He grows,
The more that I love Him, more love He bestows;
Each day is like heaven, my heart overflows,
The longer I serve Him the sweeter He grows.

23. I Love You, Lord

I love You, Lord, and I lift my voice
To worship You; O my soul, rejoice!
Take joy, my Kind, in what You hear;
May it be a sweet, sweet sound in Your ear.

24. His Name is Wonderful

His Name is Wonderful, His Name is Wonderful;
His Name is Wonderful—Jesus, my Lord.
He is the Mighty King, Master of ev'rything;
His Name is Wonderful—Jesus, my Lord.
He's the great Shepherd, the Rock of all ages,
Almighty God is He.
Bow down before Him, love and adore Him;
His Name is Wonderful—Jesus, my Lord.

25. Majesty

Majesty, worship His majesty,
Unto Jesus be all glory, honor, and praise.
Majesty, kingdom authority flow from His throne
Unto His own, His anthem raise.
So exalt, lift up on high the Name of Jesus.
Magnify, come glorify Christ Jesus, the King.
Majesty, worship His majesty;
Jesus who died, now glorified, King of all kings.

26. I Lift Your Name

Lord, my heart can grow so far away and cold;
And yet for me Your love is still the same.
Lord, I bend my knee in awe and fear of Thee,
My head bowed down in rev'rence to Your name.

I lift Your Name, Your holy Name,
Jehovah God, Elohim.
The Great I Am, the Risen Lamb,
My Comforter and King.

Lord, my heart's desire is to be filled with Spirit Fire,
My purpose is to worship You alone.
Open up my soul to worship and adore,
To be a fragrance offered to Your throne.

I lift Your Name, Your holy Name,
Jehovah God, Elohim.
The Great I Am, the Risen Lamb,
My Comforter and King.

27. Let's Just Praise the Lord

Let's just praise the Lord! Praise the Lord!
Let's just lift our hearts to heaven
And praise the Lord;
Let's just praise the Lord! Praise the Lord!
Let's just lift our hearts to heaven
And praise the Lord!

O we thank You for Your kindness,
We thank You for Your love,
We have been in heavenly places,
Felt blessings from above;
We've been sharing all the good things,
The family can afford,
Let's just turn our praise toward heaven
And praise the Lord.

Let's just praise the Lord! Praise the Lord!
Let's just lift our hearts to heaven
And praise the Lord;
Let's just praise the Lord! Praise the Lord!
Let's just lift our hearts to heaven
And praise the Lord!

28. Be Still and Know/In His Time

Be still and know that I am God.
Be still and know that I am God.
Be still and know that I am God.

In His time, In His time,
He makes all things beautiful in His time.
Lord, please show me ev'ry day
As You're teaching me Your way,
That You do just what You say,
In Your time.

I am the Lord that healeth thee.
I am the Lord that healeth thee.
I am the Lord that healeth thee.

In Thee, O Lord, I put my trust.
In Thee, O Lord, I put my trust.
In Thee, O Lord, I put my trust.

Personal Information

Judy (Heide) Miller was raised in southern Alberta, Canada. After marrying Graham, four children livened up their home. Now, nine grandchildren are a delight to the family. Most of Judy's life, she struggled with feelings of inadequacy and inferiority. When Christian counseling helped her see that she didn't need to remain stuck and that she was free to fly, her passion was to share what she learned. She has lead a women's ministry team, taught numerous Bible studies, and is presently involved in a recovery ministry in her local church. Writing about her life struggles and what she has learned through them has provided a way of encouraging others as well.

Reviews

Judy's book, "Inspirations in the Key of 'J'" has been playing music of one kind or another into our home for some time now. While the musical notes speak in one way, the written notes speak in another. Both have resonated deeply into our hearts.
Brenda Wood, Innisfil, Ontario, Canada (Conference speaker and author of Heart Felt-366 Devotions for Common Sense Living)

This is a very refreshing read. Judy has done an excellent job of taking simple observations from life and relating them to some very deep spiritual truths.
Pastor Marcel Frey, People's Church, Grande Prairie, Alberta, Canada

Judy, you have followed your desire, your dream that God has placed deeply in the recesses of your soul. You accomplished your motive—to touch lives with your ability to see a spiritual principle in your every day life of the reality of relationships, of storms, of flowers, of babies, of grandbabies. The spiritual lessons are crystal clear like the sparkles of the snow. I am honored to be your friend and have been deeply influenced by your devotional book. I am glad you stepped out on a limb and took the risk of writing a book. In doing so, you have touched many lives.
Sincerely, your friend, Eleanor Willis, Counselor, Burden Bearers, Alberta, Canada

Printed in the United States
114330LV00001B/223-240/P